T0343902

Official Cambridge Exam Preparation

COMPACT

B2 FIRST

THIRD EDITION

B2

WORKBOOK

WITH ANSWERS

WITH AUDIO

Frances Treloar

Cambridge University Press

www.cambridge.org/elt

Cambridge Assessment English

www.cambridgeenglish.org

Information on this title: www.cambridge.org/9781108921947

© Cambridge University Press and Assessment 2021

First published 2012
Second edition 2014
Third edition 2021

20 19 18 17 16 15 14 13 12 11 10 9 8 7 6

Printed in Malaysia by Vivar Printing

A catalogue record for this publication is available from the British Library

ISBN 978-1-108-92194-7 Workbook with answers

Contents

MAP OF THE UNITS

UNIT	TOPICS	GRAMMAR	VOCABULARY
1 **Living day to day**	Daily life People	Present tenses Present simple in time clauses	Adjectives ending in -ed and -ing Character adjectives Adjective prefixes and suffixes: -able, -al, dis-, -ful, -ic, im-, -ish, -itive, -ive, -ous, un-, -y
2 **Differing tastes**	Food and drink Restaurants Relationships	Past tenses	Fixed phrases
3 **Changing places**	Travel and tourism Transport Festivals and customs	Modal verbs	Dependent prepositions
4 **Getting creative**	Entertainment (film, music, arts) Leisure	Verbs followed by to + infinitive or -ing Too and enough Present perfect	Phrasal verbs with on Environmental vocabulary
5 **Making your way**	Education, study and learning Careers and jobs	Countable and uncountable nouns	
6 **Setting the pace**	Health and fitness Sport	Relative clauses (defining and non-defining)	Medical vocabulary Phrasal verbs with up
7 **Feeling the heat**	The environment The weather	Conditionals 1–3 Mixed conditionals	Collocations
8 **Moving ahead**	Science Technology	Passive forms Articles	
9 **Breaking news**	The media Celebrities	Reported speech and reporting verbs	Media vocabulary Noun suffixes
10 **Shopping around**	Shopping and consumer goods Fashion	Wish and if only Causative have and get	Clothing and shopping vocabulary Phrasal verbs with out Extreme adjectives

READING	USE OF ENGLISH	WRITING	LISTENING
Part 7: multiple matching	Part 3: word formation	Part 2 informal letter: getting ideas, informal language	Part 1: multiple-choice questions + short texts
	Part 2: open cloze	Part 2 article: narrative linking expressions	Part 2: sentence completion
	Part 1: multiple-choice cloze	Part 1 essay: linking expressions, for and against	Part 3: multiple matching
Part 6: gapped text	Part 4: key word transformations	Part 2 review: descriptive adjectives, recommendations	Part 4: multiple-choice questions + long text
Part 7: multiple matching	Part 3: word formation	Part 2 formal letter of application: formal expressions	Part 2: sentence completion
	Part 2: open cloze	Part 2 letter: informal language, purpose links	Part 1: multiple-choice questions + short texts
Part 6: gapped text	Part 4: key word transformations	Part 1 essay: contrast links	Part 3: multiple matching
Part 5: multiple-choice questions + long text	Part 1: multiple-choice cloze	Part 2 article: reason and result links, involving the reader	Part 2: sentence completion
	Part 3: word formation Part 4: key word transformations	Part 2 report: recommending and suggesting	Part 4: multiple-choice questions + long text
	Part 4: key word transformations	Part 1 essay: extreme adjectives, for and against	Part 3: multiple matching

1 Living day to day

Reading and Use of English

Part 7

1 **Look at the exam task. Answer these questions.**

1 How many short texts do you have to read?
2 What has each person written about?
3 What are the four answer choices you can give?

2 **Now do the exam task.**

Need help? Go to Quick steps page 6 in the Student's Book

✓ Exam task

You are going to read an article in which four people talk about being a foreign student. For questions **1–10**, choose from the people (**A–D**). The people may be chosen more than once.

Which person

believes she has gained a deeper understanding of various issues? `1`

is interested in the history of a feature of the city where she is studying at the moment? `2`

expresses appreciation for the convenient location of her accommodation? `3`

is aware that she may be creating a negative impression of her experience? `4`

tries to make progress in her course subject while on her way to classes? `5`

says she initially found getting from her accommodation into the city challenging? `6`

takes longer getting to classes than she needs to? `7`

mentions acquiring a skill that she regards as unnecessary? `8`

is glad that she is too busy to miss what she's left behind? `9`

felt uneasy about a teaching method at one time? `10`

Life as a foreign student

Four students talk about student life in a country that is not their own

A Emily

I'm an English university student, studying in Utrecht, Holland for one year of my law degree. My rented room is out of town, so going to and from class involves a 20-minute bike ride. Although this isn't a demanding route, cycling it was tough at first as I was so unfit. Now, I can see that commuting to uni and cycling into town for things like my weekly Dutch lessons have made me much fitter. Learning Dutch is interesting, but hardly essential since everyone here speaks such good English! In town, I also sometimes meet up with friends in Utrecht's amazing cafés after uni classes. I particularly like the cafés in the converted industrial buildings by the canal, which have a long and fascinating past that I've enjoyed researching online. At weekends, I go with friends to places like the Domtoren, Utrecht's famous tower. The views from the top are stunning. All in all, I'd highly recommend studying abroad.

B Meera

I'm from India, and I'm studying economics at Harvard University, USA. Since being here, I've had no time to be homesick or think about much except my classes and coping with the workload, which is a good thing. My classes start at 8.45, and then it's constant classes and helping researchers until 6 pm, with ten minutes for lunch and perhaps an hour in the library for my own coursework. In the evening, I might have to take a progress test, get through several books, and work on assignments. I realise it must sound like I'm living in a highly stressed state, but in fact that's not how it feels because I'm so delighted to be here. I find the whole experience really stimulating and rewarding.

Grammar

Present tenses

1 ⊙ **Some of these sentences written by exam candidates contain mistakes. Correct any mistakes, using the present simple or present continuous.**

1 Petra is belonging to the only sports club in our town.
2 I'll do the washing up when you'll leave.
3 We're having a really enjoyable time here in the city.
4 Every day they are sitting at their desks for at least six hours.
5 When you will visit my sister, please take her this present from me.
6 The horses are needing their food at five o'clock, but they almost never get it on time.
7 Nowadays, it becomes increasingly difficult to find a really wild place to go hiking.
8 I promise that I'll explain the problem to Mike when I meet with him.

C Elsa

I'm from Sweden, but at the moment I'm living in Singapore, doing a business degree. About ten minutes before classes start each morning, I stuff my laptop into my bag, and head to uni, feeling huge relief that my halls of residence are just five minutes away on foot. Most often, our classes are seminars with the professor. Although the discussions in these are usually full of interesting insights from classmates as well as the prof, this type of session, where students question everything, made me uncomfortable at first and I was concerned I'd learn nothing! I'm pleased to say I was completely wrong. Although core classes end at midday, I often have to attend meetings later about team projects, and go to electives – additional classes usually unrelated to core subjects. I've done several fascinating electives, such as one on Japanese social history. Being here has shown me how narrow my thinking was. I've become much more knowledgeable about different cultures, politics and lifestyles.

D Melanie

I'm an Australian studying French in Nancy, France. It was a while before I really felt settled here. Having lived in a small outback town for most of my life, French city life felt pretty overwhelming. Now, I love it. Every morning I set off for the school, which could just be a ten-minute walk from my apartment, but is often more like half an hour because I take different routes, exploring the historic streets of Nancy. As I walk, I listen to amusing French podcasts to improve my listening skills. They also make me feel calmer about the day ahead. Since I'm doing an intensive language course, some exhausting days I have six hours of French classes. I only have two hours on Thursday and Friday though, so generally feel a lot more chilled out by the weekend. After classes, I meet up with friends in restaurants or work on my French.

2 Complete these sentences with the present simple or present continuous form of these verbs. Use each verb only once.

end	not shout	own	stay	take	try

1 I hate novels that .... without explaining why things happened.
2 Debra's away this week. She .... at her parents' place in the mountains.
3 Teachers tend to get better results if they .... at their pupils.
4 I'm tired of eating in the canteen, so I .... a packed lunch to work.
5 A footballer from Manchester United .... that huge house over there.
6 Don't come in here! I .... to clean the floor.

Listening

Part 1

1 Look at questions 1–4 in the exam task. Answer these questions.

1 How many speakers will you hear?
2 Will they be female or male voices?
3 What is the situation?
4 What is the focus, e.g. place, opinion, of the question?

2 🔊 **01** Now listen and do the exam task.

Need help? Go to Quick steps page 9 in the Student's Book

✓ Exam task

You will hear people talking in four different situations (in the exam you will hear eight). For questions **1–4**, choose the best answer (**A**, **B** or **C**).

1 You hear a woman talking to a friend in a restaurant. What does the woman want to avoid doing?
   A driving home through slow traffic
   B using public transport to get home
   C returning home that evening

2 You hear a father and his daughter chatting about this weekend. How does the daughter feel about this weekend?
   A She is concerned about how much she will have to do for her grandma.
   B She is looking forward to spending time with her grandma.
   C She is hoping to do some baking with her grandma.

3 You hear a man leaving a phone message for his sister. Why is he calling her?
   A to invite her to join him on vacation
   B to accept her offer of accommodation
   C to confirm some arrangements for a trip

4 You overhear a man and a woman talking in a shopping centre. What do they agree to do now?
   A find somewhere to have a meal
   B go to the department store café
   C see if they can get something in the sales

Reading and Use of English

1 ⊙ **Correct the mistakes in these sentences written by exam candidates. Add a prefix and/or a suffix to the underlined words.**

1 He's your father, so of course he is <u>worry</u> about you when you have problems.
2 When Henrik became a senior manager, he felt more <u>stressy</u> about work.
3 The most <u>attraction</u> courses I've seen so far are all in London.
4 After the long silence, there was a sudden scream, and we were all <u>terrorised</u>.
5 This essay is totally <u>inacceptable</u> because it doesn't answer the question at all.
6 It was really <u>surprised</u> to find out that our school was once a luxury hotel.
7 The stadium was incredibly <u>crowdy</u> so we couldn't get near the stage.
8 Having some time off work will be really <u>enjoyful</u>.
9 The conference I went to was extremely <u>unorganised</u> and uninteresting.
10 The city's fantastic art gallery is full of <u>impressing</u> paintings and sculptures.

Part 3

2 **Look at the exam task example (0) and answer these questions.**

1 What kind of word is needed in the gap: an adjective, noun or adverb?
2 Does the word describe how people feel about something, or what has caused them to feel that?
3 Does the given word need a suffix or a prefix?
4 What other change to the given word is needed?

3 Now do the exam task.

Need help? Go to Quick steps page 12 in the Student's Book

✓ Exam task

For questions **1–8**, read the text below. Use the word given in capitals at the end of some of the lines to form a word that fits in the gap in the same line. There is an example at the beginning (**0**).

Example: 0 CHALLENGING

The effects of social media

Today, it is **(0)** .... to imagine a world without social media, which is used by around 3.8 billion people **(1)** .... Its main use is to establish and maintain	CHALLENGE
	GLOBE
(2) .... and family ties. Though people find certain aspects of online social communication	FRIEND
(3) ...., there's growing evidence of its positive effects.	WORRY
For example, a study of 1,000 teenagers aged between 13 and 17, found that one in five believed they had more **(4)** .... communicating on social media than in more traditional ways. 28% of them also expressed the	CONFIDENT
(5) .... that social media made them more outgoing, and over half said it improved their relationships.	BELIEVE
(6) .... have also focused specifically on students and social media use. They have shown that students who use social media frequently have better memories and feel more **(7)** .... with their academic subject. Social media users also tend to be more innovative, possibly because social media provides such a wide and	RESEARCH
	INVOLVE
(8) .... range of ways to learn and research.	VARY

Writing

Part 2 informal email

1 Look at the exam task and answer these questions.

1 Who is the email to and who wrote it?
2 What does he want you to write about?
3 Underline the informal language he uses.

✓ Exam task

Here is part of an email you have received from Sam, an English-speaking friend.

> I met up with Leona yesterday. She's a good mate, but very different from me in many ways – she's six years older than me and loads more sensible, etc. etc!
>
> Can you tell me about a friend of yours who's different to you, and explain how they're different?
>
> Look forward to hearing from you soon.

Write your **email** to Sam in **140–190** words. Do not write any addresses.

2 Read the model email and respond to the following.

1 Complete the words in *italics*, adding a letter or letters.
2 What answers does Francisco give to Sam's questions?
3 Find and underline examples of informal language.

Hi Sam,

Thanks for your email. It was great to hear all your awesome news.

I think it's really **(1)** *interest*..... that you have a close friend who's so different from you. Most of my friends are quite similar to me, but there's one who's not. His name's Juan, and I've **(2)** *know*..... him since we were kids. But a few years ago he moved to Brazil, a long way from Mexico, where I live. He's the same age as me, but he does things that are quite **(3)** .....*usual* for people our age. When I'm not studying, I like to do fun things, But Juan's a more serious kind of guy. He's much more passionate than me, and one of the things he's passionate about is global warming. He's very **(4)** *concern*..... about its effect on the world, so he often **(5)** *take*..... part in demonstrations and **(6)** *write*..... to politicians about the issue. I admire what he does – he's really cool. But as I'm in my final year at uni, I'm concentrating on **(7)** *get*..... a degree right now, and don't feel I have much time for stuff like that.

Write back soon,

Francisco

3 Plan and write your email to Sam. If possible, use some of Francisco's expressions, grammar structures and vocabulary.

Need help? Go to Quick steps page 13 and the Writing bank page 120 in the Student's Book

2 Differing tastes

Listening

Part 2

1 Look at the exam task. Answer these questions.

1 Look at the instructions. Who is the speaker in this task? What is the review about?

2 Look at the gaps for questions 1–10. Which gap or gaps can be filled by the following?

a a role
b a place
c a product
d a length of time
e an adjective

2 🔊 02 Now listen and do the exam task.

Need help? Go to Quick steps page 16 in the Student's Book

✓ Exam task

You will hear a radio presenter reviewing a biography of a chef. For questions **1–10**, complete the sentences with a word or short phrase.

1 The presenter thinks that everyone will find Kwame's biography a very .... book.

2 Kwame studied for a while at a ...., which he was forced to leave.

3 When he went to Louisiana, he was hired to work in the kitchens of a ...., which was where he began his career in cooking.

4 In 2010, Kwame went back to New York and became a .... in a restaurant.

5 Kwame set up a catering business with money he earned from selling .... on the subway.

6 Kwame's restaurant, Shaw Bijou, was only open for .... before it went out of business.

7 Shaw Bijou had a key .... who was responsible for the decision to close it down.

8 The speaker says that what motivated Kwame was a .... that was always with him.

9 Kwame's current restaurant is in a .... in Washington.

10 Next week on this programme, the type of book being reviewed will be a............................, written by an Italian chef.

Grammar

a   b   c

Past tenses

1 ⊘ Correct the mistakes in these sentences using suitable past tenses. In sentences 3 and 8 more than one answer is possible.

1 When we chatted in the café, I didn't notice someone stealing my bag.

2 During the phone call, Felicity was asking him to go camping at the weekend.

3 Before I had a computer, I was looking things up in books.

4 I ran to the cinema and arrived at 7.15 but the film already started.

5 My dad didn't used to have dinner with us very often because he worked long hours.

6 My aunt's beautiful antique vase broke while I washed it.

7 The glass on the table was containing a strange green liquid.

8 After Greg had working in the shop for several years, he became the manager.

9 When Nick arrived at the party it was late and most of the other guests went home.

2 Choose the correct answer to complete the text.

Photographs of food

When I put 'photos of desserts' into a search engine this morning, I got hundreds of millions of results. When I **(1) was having / had had** dinner with a friend last week, he did not start eating each dish until he **(2) had taken / took** endless shots of it. Whereas the focus of dining **(3) was being / used to be** the taste of the food, its appearance and presentation has become more and more important. Taking photos of food has become part of the dining experience, and many restaurants use photos as a key marketing tool. So how **(4) was all this starting / did all this start**?

The earliest photos of food date back to the early days of photography in the nineteenth century. At that time, photographers **(5) were trying / tried** to establish photography as a serious art form. During the 1860s, for example, a photographer called Roger Fenton **(6) would photograph / had photographed** richly detailed scenes of food, which imitated the 'still life' displays of objects so brilliantly painted by the Dutch masters. He **(7) produced / had been producing** large prints of these to be hung as decorative works of art. Up until the 20th century and the rise of mass-produced photographic prints, this type of print **(8) had been selling / had been sold** well. However, with this and other developments in technology, the style and function of food photography began to change dramatically.

Rather than being works of art, photos of food in the beginning and middle of the twentieth century more commonly had functional purposes such as illustrations in recipe books. For many years, these photos **(9) would be taken / were taken** from the point of view of the eater. Food was laid out on the table, and photos were shot from above, looking down, with the plates clearly separated. Towards the end of the century, romantic lighting, lower angles and adding decorative objects **(10) had been / was** the trend. Nowadays, a lot of Western food photography aims to display food as simply and naturally as possible, with very few objects included.

Reading and Use of English

Part 2

1 Look at the exam task and answer the following questions.

1 Read the title. What tenses do you expect to see in the text? What do you know about the topic before reading the text?

2 Look at each gap in the text and find one where the following will fit: a superlative adjective, a relative pronoun, past tense forms.

2 Now do the exam task.

Need help? Go to Quick steps page 20 in the Student's Book

☑ Exam task

For questions **1–8**, read the text below and try to think of the word which best fits each gap. Use **only** one word in each gap. There is an example at the beginning (**0**).

Example: 0 *WHOSE*

A short history of the olive

The olive, **(0)** .... botanical name is Olea europaea, is a small tree in the family Oleaceae. It now grows in many parts of the world, from the Mediterranean area to **(1)** .... far east as China. However, it probably came originally from the region **(2)** .... is now Iran, Syria and Palestine, and then spread to the more western Mediterranean.

The olive is very old. In fact, it is one of the world's **(3)** .... ancient cultivated trees. By 3,000 BCE, olives **(4)** .... already reached the Greek island of Crete, and were being grown in **(5)** .... to make oil. Olive crops may have been a source of the great wealth accumulated by the Minoan Kingdom on Crete (2700 – 1100 BCE). Olives dating from 2,000 BCE have also **(6)** .... found in Egyptian tombs. Olive culture **(7)** .... passed on by the early Greeks to the Romans, and as the Roman Empire grew, so **(8)** .... the world's love of the olive.

Vocabulary

Fixed phrases

Complete the sentences with words from the box.

alone	attracted	company	ease	fed	heart
nerves	propose	shape	side	sight	touch

1 Jimmy's in pretty bad .... because he's been ill and unable to exercise.

2 The play's main character breaks his lover's .... when he runs away to sea.

3 I'm .... up with this cold living room – we must get the heating fixed.

4 I just want to be left .... – I don't want to talk about it.

5 My advice is, only .... to Jasmine if you think she'll say yes!

6 I've never been .... to men with beards – I prefer the clean-shaven look.

7 My speaking examiner was nice – he really made me feel at .... before we started.

8 Drivers who don't consider other road users really get on my ....

9 I don't feel great, but I'll come to the birthday dinner – I can't let the .... down!

10 When you move to the US, let's make sure we don't lose ....

11 My parents were away, so my cousin came and kept me .... in the evenings.

12 At first ...., the hotel looked a bit shabby, but inside it was lovely.

Writing

1 Look at the exam task and answer the following questions.

1 What kind of text will you write, and what is it for?
2 Which two things do you need to describe?

☑ Exam task

You have seen this announcement in an international magazine.

> Write an article for us with this title:
> **A celebration meal**
> Tell us about what you were celebrating and what happened at the meal.
> We will publish the three most interesting articles next month.

Write your **article** in **140–190** words.

2 Quickly read the model article and answer these questions.

1 What does the first paragraph do?
   A explains the title of the article
   B introduces the event in the article
2 What was the writer celebrating?
3 What happened at the meal?

3 Look at the model article again. Complete it with the linking expressions in the box.

> Although   Before long   For this reason
> In the meantime   Once   The moment

4 Plan and write your article. Include what the task asks for.

Need help? Go to Quick steps page 21 and the Writing bank page 124 in the Student's Book

A celebration meal

Nowadays, people generally go out for meals more often than when I was young. The only time our family would eat in a restaurant when I was growing up was when there was a family celebration of some kind, like a birthday or wedding anniversary. **(1)** ...., such occasions were very memorable.

One great celebration meal I remember was for my grandad's seventieth birthday. My mum organised it, and Grandad didn't know anything about it. On the day, my parents, sisters, uncles, aunts and cousins arrived at a posh restaurant before Grandad, and waited for him to arrive. **(2)** ...., my gran was driving Grandad to the restaurant. She'd told him they were going to have a quiet meal together, just the two of them.

(3) ...., we saw them arrive outside the restaurant. We were so excited! **(4)** .... they entered the room, we all yelled 'surprise!' Grandad nearly fell over when he saw us all there!

(5) .... he'd got over the shock, he was totally thrilled that we'd all come to celebrate with him.

(6) .... it was a wonderful occasion, I don't remember anything about what we ate!

3 Changing places

a   b

c   d

Listening

Part 3

1 Read the exam task instructions.

1 What is the topic of the five monologues?
2 How many of the options A–H <u>won't</u> you need to use?

2 What do you think you should do before you listen to Speaker 1?

3 🔊 03 Now listen and do the exam task.

Need help? Go to Quick steps page 24 in the Student's Book

✓ Exam task

You will hear five short extracts in which people are talking about a group cycle trip they went on. For questions **1–5**, choose from the list (**A–H**) what each speaker said about the trip they went on. Use the letters only once. There are three extra letters which you do not need to use.

A The pace we rode at was just right for me.
B I particularly enjoyed meeting local people.
C It was worth riding the difficult sections to get the views.
D I got on really well with the rest of the tour group.
E I was surprised at how attractive the landscape was.
F I was relieved that the route was not too busy.
G I nearly gave up a couple of times.
H The encouragement others gave me was helpful.

Speaker 1 **1**

Speaker 2 **2**

Speaker 3 **3**

Speaker 4 **4**

Speaker 5 **5**

Grammar

Modal verbs

1 Complete the sentences with a modal verb from the box.

can't have   could   don't have to   might have
need to   should have   shouldn't have

1 Georgiou is allergic to nuts, so he .... eaten your peanuts; it's impossible.
2 It's OK, we .... go shopping tomorrow – I've bought what I wanted online.
3 You .... turned your phone off before the play started!
4 If you're free, we .... go and see Kate's band tonight – they're playing in town.
5 Leah .... given her grandson all those sweets – they made him sick!
6 I .... go and study in the library tomorrow, so I can't come to basketball practice.
7 I'm not sure why that meat tasted so strange – it .... been in the freezer too long, or perhaps I didn't cook it long enough.

2 ◉ Correct the exam candidates' mistakes underlined in these sentences. There may be more than one possible answer.

1 He <u>hasn't to</u> explain his actions, but I wish he would.
2 The shop assistant gave us instructions on using the food mixer so we <u>needn't to look</u> it up online.
3 I will send you a list of sights you <u>can</u> find interesting in Porto.
4 Freddie <u>must</u> buy a jumper when he was in Malta because he forgot to pack one.
5 My grandma lived in this street as a girl – it's funny to think that she <u>could play</u> in one of those gardens!
6 Now Nick has retired he <u>must not</u> wear a suit every day – he's really happy about that!
7 When I got to the shop, I'd forgotten what I needed – I <u>should write</u> a list.
8 Elsa <u>must not have</u> spent all morning cleaning the house because her visitors didn't come.

Vocabulary

1 ◉ In each of these sentences written by exam candidates, the dependent preposition is either wrong or missing. Correct these mistakes.

1 I've had no response of the question I sent my tutor.
2 The class is definitely in need for more listening practice before the exam.
3 My nephew is totally obsessed to dinosaurs at the moment.
4 Jim's tired but it's got nothing to do about studying – he went to an all-night party on Saturday.
5 After I saw a documentary on global warming, I've become much more conscious with how much energy I'm using.
6 Ask Dougie to write your reference – he knows how capable for doing the job you are.
7 I'm emailing with regard of a recent purchase in your store.
8 How about playing football rather than tennis? It's a sport I'm more familiar.

2 Read the sentences and use the missing words to complete the crossword. All these words are in the Reading task on Page 23 of the Student's Book.

Across

1 Living in a small rural .... has advantages and disadvantages.
3 If you want to do something useful in your free time, why not become a .... for a charity?
5 The play was produced by the school drama club in .... with the local theatre.
7 To reduce global warming, everyone needs to think about adopting a more .... lifestyle.

Down

2 Henry sold his antique car because of the high .... costs.
4 The government is planning to launch a healthy eating .... in schools soon.
6 The restaurant has recently been .... and now looks better than ever.
8 Jimmy's told Goldie not to get him a present, but she's .... that she will get him one. There's no changing her mind.

Reading and Use of English

1 Look at the exam task example (0) and decide if these sentences are true or false.

1 The answer options are all nouns with closely related meanings.
2 There are two correct answers.
3 Choosing the answer depends on knowing some grammar rules.

2 Two gaps involve dependent prepositions. Circle the two gaps.

3 Now do the exam task.

Need help? Go to Quick steps page 28 in the Student's Book

✓ Exam task

For questions **1–8**, read the text below and decide which answer (**A**, **B**, **C** or **D**) best fits each gap. There is an example at the beginning (**0**).

Example: 0   **A** type   **B** track   **C** way   **D** route

Tips for planning
a rail trip around Europe

Travelling around Europe by train is a straightforward, relatively cheap **(0)** ......C...... of visiting lots of different countries. Starting in northern Italy, you could be in Germany, the Czech Republic or Austria in just a few hours, for example. **(1)** ...., when planning a trip it's advisable to **(2)** .... the number of places you visit, otherwise you'll see little except the inside of a train. To give yourself enough time to **(3)** .... everything a large city has to offer, you need to stay at least three nights.
Once you've **(4)** .... on where you want to go, it's essential to become **(5)** .... with the relevant train routes and timetables. When you look at a map, it might seem that two places look **(6)** .... close, but the journey time turns out to be **(7)** .... long. By the time you've changed trains several times, you may have lost a lot of your valuable sightseeing time. Careful planning **(8)** .... you get the right balance between travel and exploring.

1 **A** Furthermore	**B** Instead	**C** Therefore	**D** However
2 **A** tighten	**B** limit	**C** suspend	**D** decline
3 **A** explore	**B** learn	**C** find	**D** realise
4 **A** selected	**B** settled	**C** picked	**D** opted
5 **A** knowledgeable	**B** accustomed	**C** familiar	**D** aware
6 **A** a bit	**B** fairly	**C** slightly	**D** a little
7 **A** completely	**B** extremely	**C** absolutely	**D** totally
8 **A** ensures	**B** provides	**C** establishes	**D** maintains

Writing

1 Look at the exam task and answer these questions.

1 What question should the essay answer?
2 Whose ideas does an English teacher want to read?
3 Is your answer to the question 'yes', 'no', or 'yes and no'? Why?

✓ Exam task

In your English class, you have been talking about the advantages and disadvantages of schools taking their students away on trips. Now, your English teacher has asked you to write an essay.

Write an essay using all the notes and give reasons for your point of view.

> *Should schools take their students away on trips?*
>
> Notes
> Write about:
> 1 what students could learn
> 2 the cost
> 3 your own idea

Write your **essay** in **140–190** words. You must use grammatically correct sentences with accurate spelling and punctuation in an appropriate style.

2 Read the model essay and do the following:

1 Decide what's wrong with the underlined words/ phrases, and replace them.
2 Circle the linking phrases.
3 Find the three parts which the task notes say you must include.

> One possible argument against schools taking their students away on trips is the cost. No matter how short or uncomplicated the trip may be, there are travel costs involved in taking a group of young people away. If children's parents are unable to pay for them, the school has to fund them, and this may take money away from other parts of the curriculum.
>
> However, this disadvantage is far outweighed by the the advantages. Firstly, and most importantly, going out of school to experience cultural events, do new activities or visit spectacular natural landscapes is extremely educational for young people. <u>It's</u> a much more effective way of learning about the world than reading about such <u>stuff</u> in a book or on screen. Secondly, trips are vital for some children, as they are their only opportunity to travel and see new things. Finally, children need stimulation to stay motivated to learn, so providing a change from the routine of school life is <u>really cool</u> for them.
>
> In summary, my answer to this question is yes. I strongly believe that schools should take their students away on as many trips as possible.

3 Plan and write your essay. Don't forget to use some linking words and expressions.

Need help? Go to Quick steps page 29 and the Writing bank page 118 in the Student's Book

Reading and Use of English

Part 6

1 Quickly read the first two lines of the text. What does the writer do?

2 Now do the exam task. Use the underlined words in the options A–G to help you find the answers.

Need help? Go to Quick steps page 30 in the Student's Book

✓ **Exam task**

You are going to read an article about becoming a scenic painter. Six sentences have been removed from the article. Choose from the sentences **A–G** the one which fits each gap (**1–6**). There is one extra sentence which you do not need to use.

Becoming a scenic painter

For 25 years now, I've been a 'scenic painter'. This means it's been my job to paint the background scenery for productions such as plays and films.

To most people, the role of the scenic painter is an invisible one. Who thinks much about the scenery when they go to see a movie or a play? **1** ☐ On trips to the theatre, I never considered the scenery, even though I decided in my teens that the only career I was interested in was one that involved painting or drawing. And I'm not unusual: all my scenic-painter colleagues started off as portrait painters, illustrators or costume designers. None came directly from education into scenic painting.

It was pure luck that got me into it. In my final year of a degree in fine art, I heard that a scenic artist was setting up a studio near where I was living. I contacted her to enquire about the possibility of some kind of training just as she was looking for an assistant. I got the job mainly because I was keen, had a strong portfolio of paintings, and was ready to work hard. **2** ☐ Essentially, I was the right person in the right place at the right time.

Working as an assistant to an expert scenic painter gave me the perfect base for my career. **3** ☐ This involved learning to use many different kinds of paints, frames and styles, and being guided in experimentation. But in addition to these practical aspects, my boss built my confidence and introduced me to some very useful contacts.

Learning on the job, as I did, is one of several different ways into the industry. If I'd been more aware of this line of work at a younger age, I could have gone straight from school to do an undergraduate degree in it, or done a post graduate course later. **4** ☐ Nowadays, there's an extremely wide range of university courses on offer, which either specialise in three years training for scenic painting or include it as part of a more general course.

Another path to being a scenic painter for a few lucky people is a formal apprenticeship. I would have loved to do the one offered by the Royal Opera House, for example. Their two-year scenic art apprenticeship is a great combination of on-the-job learning and training in the core techniques. **5** ☐ Most aspiring scenic painters realise it would make the perfect start to a career: learning in one of the world's best studios, gaining industry contacts and being paid while you're gaining all these benefits!

I never regret the career path I took, however, and wouldn't change any of it. The experience I gained in my first job enabled me to get work in a big London theatre. After about ten years I went freelance, working for many different companies, supplying scenery art for all kinds of theatre, ballet, opera and musicals. **6** ☐ Other great aspects are the creativity involved and the fact it's so absorbing. A twelve-hour day of work to finish a project often flashes by in what seems like a moment.

A However, the choices available were more limited back then.

B As you might expect, the main element was getting trained in the technical side of the job.

C This variety is one of the things I love about my job.

D This approach was difficult, but all my hard work paid off in the end.

E I certainly didn't before I became the person creating it.

F The fact that I was local was also a big plus.

G It goes without saying that competition for a place on such a scheme is tough.

Grammar

a   b   c

too and *enough*,
present perfect,
verb + infinitive / *-ing*

⦿ Correct the mistakes in these sentences written by exam candidates. In some cases, more than one answer is possible.

1 Don't get any more cheese – I already have bought lots.
2 I dislike to sleep during the day – it just feels wrong!
3 If you don't hurry up, we won't have enough time for eat a meal before the film starts.
4 Some new neighbours just have moved into the flat next door.
5 I'll start the book you recommended when I've finished to read this one.
6 They haven't still met Patrick's new girlfriend.
7 We'll have to book a hotel – it's too far for us going just for the day.
8 Greta regrets to give away her guitar. She'd like to

take it up again now.
9 I like my new flat, but I miss to be able to walk to the shops like I could from my old flat.
10 Pedro's really unfit because he hasn't done any exercise since a few years.

Reading and Use of English

Part 4

1 Look at the exam task instructions and answer these questions.

1 What is the maximum number of words you should write in the gap?
2 Look at the example. What changes had to be made for the answer?

2 Now do the exam task.

Need help? Go to Quick steps page 35 in the Student's Book

✓ Exam task

For questions **1–6**, complete the second sentence so that it has a similar meaning to the first sentence, using the word given. **Do not change the word given.** You must use between **two** and **five** words, including the word given. Here is an example (**0**).

Example:

0 Even though we set off at 6.30 am, it was too late to avoid the rush hour traffic.
EARLY
Even though we set off at 6.30 am, it
WASN'T / WAS NOT EARLY ENOUGH to avoid
the rush hour traffic.

1 They got married about ten years ago.
FOR
They ....
about ten years.

2 The rock star stopped performing live in 2018.
SINCE
The rock star
.... 2018.

3 Jasmine ran and only stopped when she was too tired to continue.
WENT
Jasmine ....
she was too tired to continue.

4 Amy's happy to drive if you don't want to.
MIND
Amy ....if you
don't want to.

5 These instructions aren't simple enough for me to follow.
COMPLICATED
These instructions
....for me to
follow.

6 I gave up learning Japanese writing after trying for three months.
ATTEMPTED
I ....in
Japanese but gave up after three months.

Listening

Part 4

1 Read the exam task. Are the following true or false? Give reasons for your answers.

Task instructions

1 You will hear just one person speaking in the recording.
2 In the recording, Toby's friend is talking about her job.
3 Each question has four answer options.

What we can learn before listening

4 Toby works for a company called Donut.
5 Toby works in a large team.
6 Toby enjoys his job.

2 🔊 04 **Now listen and do the exam task.**

Need help? Go to Quick steps page 32 in the Student's Book

☑ Exam task

You will hear a man called Toby Jackson telling a friend about his job as an animator, someone who creates pictures and makes them into cartoons or videos. For questions **1–7**, choose the best answer (**A**, **B** or **C**).

1 Toby says that his current company, Donut, specialises in animations used in
   A sources of government information.
   B commercial advertising campaigns.
   C educational materials.

2 How does Toby feel about the research he is doing for his work?
   A impatient to get it finished
   B grateful to be learning from specialists
   C pleased to be gaining some in-depth knowledge

3 Toby likes working in a small team because he is
   A involved in every stage of big projects.
   B allowed to work alone on some parts of projects.
   C supported by colleagues throughout each project.

4 Toby finds his work satisfying because what he creates is
   A totally original.
   B highly skilled.
   C constantly improving.

5 What does Toby say about putting fun into his work?
   A The nature of the work usually makes it easy.
   B He sometimes forgets to focus enough on it.
   C In certain situations it's hard to achieve.

6 What does Toby say about new projects?
   A He is not good at starting them off.
   B He dislikes being in charge of the initial stages.
   C Developing the story takes him a long time.

7 Toby thinks that advances in technology mean
   A the only limit on what to animate is his imagination.
   B it is virtually impossible to keep up with the speed of change.
   C animators can be selective about what they use.

Vocabulary

Two-part verbs with *on*

Match the two halves of the sentences.

1 Please just hang ☐

2 Tom won't be able to walk tomorrow if he carries ☐

3 I've got an essay to do so I want to focus ☐

4 Marcus is nice – if you want a cheerful companion you can always rely ☐

5 That fish is not ready yet – keep ☐

6 Ollie and Greta need to decide ☐

7 The factory is taking ☐

8 The teacher wants Dan to attend the extra lesson but she won't insist ☐

9 Eric spends a lot of his free time working ☐

10 In his books, the novelist draws ☐

11 Matt gave up collecting watches and moved ☐

12 This car is environmentally friendly – it runs ☐

a   on running that fast.
b   on him going.
c   on frying it for a bit longer.
d   on to antique books.
e   on an old car he bought last year.
f   on extra office staff.
g   on a minute. I'm not ready to go yet.
h   on electricity.
i   on finishing that before I start planning my weekend.
j   on a date for the wedding.
k   on him.
l   on his childhood experiences.

Writing

1 Look at the exam task and answer these questions.

1 What must your review be about?
2 Where will people read your review?
3 What must you include in your review?

✓ Exam task

An art website is looking for reviews of places to see art. You decide to write a review for the website. Describe a place where you have seen art and say what you think of it. Would you recommend this place to other people?

Write your **review** in **140–190** words.

2 Read the model essay and write the correct paragraph number.

a   This paragraph tells you the positive points about the place. ☐

b   This paragraph tells you a few basic facts about the place. ☐

c   This gives you a recommendation. ☐

d   This paragraph tells you a couple of negative things about the place. ☐

Sculptures in the forest

1 I recently visited Greybeck Forest with a friend to see the sculptures that have been put there. There are thirty sculptures in total, and you can walk around them all in about two hours.

2 Greybeck forest is <u>nice</u>, and if you are interested in nature, you will enjoy seeing all the different trees, flowers and birds that live there. The sculptures are a <u>nice</u> mixture of different shapes, styles, and sizes, from some <u>small</u> metal bells hanging from a tree, to a <u>big</u> wooden circle. A big part of the fun is finding the sculptures in the forest, following a free map that you can get from the visitor centre. The only thing you have to pay for is the parking for your car.

3 The cost of parking is quite high, which is one of the only downsides to this place. The other downside is the walk. It took us two hours to see all the sculptures, and the path was quite <u>difficult</u> in places. So it may not be <u>good</u> for everyone.

4 However, if you enjoy walking and art, I recommend seeing Greybeck Forest sculptures. It is a <u>nice</u> place to spend a sunny afternoon.

3 Replace the underlined adjectives with the following:

> beautiful   fascinating   huge   steep
> suitable   tiny   wonderful

4 Now do the exam task. Write about anywhere you like: an area of street art, galleries, school exhibitions, art on public transport or in city centres, etc.

Need help? Go to Quick steps page 37 and the Writing bank page 122 in the Student's Book

Reading and Use of English

Part 7

1 Write down some reasons why someone might want to be a doctor.

2 Look at the exam task without reading the texts. Are these statements true or false? Explain why the false ones are not true.

1 The writers of the four texts are all doctors now.
2 When you read, you will learn mainly about what they want to do in the future.
3 You should find just one answer in each of the texts.
4 The questions are in the same order that the answers occur in the texts.

3 Read the questions for this task and underline the key points you will need to look for when you read.

4 Now do the exam task.

Need help? Go to Quick steps page 38 in the Student's Book

☑ Exam task

You are going to read a magazine article in which four doctors talk about why they chose a career in medicine. For questions **1–10**, choose from the doctors (**A–D**). The sections may be chosen more than once.

Which doctor

says she joined the medical profession unusually late in life?	1
mentions how she felt at the beginning of her training?	2
mentions how she was encouraged to become a doctor in a way that was not obvious at the time?	3
says she has never considered any other career?	4
struggled against her parents when she was younger?	5
changed her mind about her career after hearing someone speak about their work?	6
admits that she had an uncommon free-time activity when she was a child?	7
says she continues to be inspired by other doctors?	8
says that certain personal qualities are essential to her role?	9
mentions someone recommending that she began a career in medicine?	10

A Olivia

I grew up as the only daughter of two successful doctors who set me extremely high standards for everything I did, from doing the washing up to passing my exams. I fought this all through my teens, but now I can see the benefits of setting yourself ambitious goals. In this job you have to be disciplined and extremely hardworking. I didn't realise it at the time, but my mum and dad were also inspiring me to go into medicine from a very young age. Over the years, the most powerful impact was made not by giving me information or practical help, but simply through the passion with which they spoke about their work and their patients. As well as this, though, they did take me to their hospital to show me what they had to do as doctors, and Mum arranged work experience for me there before I went to university.

B Nadia

When I was about twelve, my younger brother developed a health condition which meant he had lots of contact with doctors. I've always been very curious, and I bombarded my parents constantly with questions about my brother's illness. In their answers, I got many insights into what the job entailed. However, if anything, this experience put me off a career in medicine because the amount to learn seemed overwhelming. Possibly as a result of this, I was more mature than most people when I came to medicine as I'd already done an arts degree, got married and started work in a library. Then I lost my job, and my husband, who's a doctor himself, suggested I look into medical training because he thought I'd make a good doctor. I couldn't think of a reason not to and now, I'm loving every minute of being in this profession.

C Emma

I'm often asked what made me follow in my father's footsteps and become a doctor. My dad's the son of immigrants, and he was the first doctor in his family. Although his parents pushed him really hard to do well at school, that didn't bother him because he enjoyed science, maths and languages, and rarely had any difficulty with his studies because he's exceptionally clever. I enjoyed school too. As far back as I can remember, I've always just assumed I was going to be a doctor. The only subjects that really interested me were the sciences, and on weekends, Dad would take me with him to work at the hospital. It all seemed perfectly natural then, but in retrospect, it was a rather bizarre way for a young girl to spend her free time!

D Marianne

Essentially, what motivated me to become a doctor was the desire to help others. I've always wanted to work in a job that was really worthwhile, and what could be more so than this? However, as I didn't have any role models for this calling in my family, I thought when I was about 15 that I might like to be a youth worker or a social worker. Then we had a visitor at school giving a talk about his job as a cancer specialist. That focused me on medicine, and as soon as I started medical school, I knew I'd chosen the right career for me. That's where I not only learnt the practical skills, but I also started to make the connections with patients that make this job so rewarding. And now, whenever I work with young medical students and newly qualified doctors, I'm reminded of my initial motivations. Their joy, passion and desire to serve others helps me maintain enthusiasm for my work.

Grammar

Countable and uncountable nouns

◉ Some of these sentences written by exam candidates contain mistakes.
Correct any mistakes and tick (✓) the sentences that are correct.

1 Our biology teacher always gives us a lot of homeworks to do over the weekend.
2 It's OK, I don't need any helps. I can change the tyre myself.
3 We did some research into various marine mammals for our project.
4 I think studying online increases our knowledges more quickly than reading books.
5 You need to get work experience at a scientific institution such as a university.
6 I'd like some advices about the best way to make a lemon tart.
7 Plastic rubbishes can be found in almost every part of every ocean.
8 I don't get much time for leisures because of my long working day.
9 Average earning in this country are increasing more slowly than the price of food.
10 The only means of crossing the channel to the island is by ferry.

Reading and Use of English

Part 3

1 Read the title of the exam text only and complete these predictions.

1 I expect the text to contain vocabulary relating to *work / education*.

2 I expect the text to be about *a specific career change / career changes in general*.

2 Look at the example (0) in the text and choose the correct option to complete these sentences.

1 The answer is *a countable noun / an uncountable noun*.

2 The answer is *singular / plural*.

3 Look at the words before and after the example gap (0) in the text. Underline two words which show you the answer is plural or singular.

4 Now do the exam task.

Need help? Go to Quick steps page 44 in the Student's Book

✓ Exam task

For questions **1–8**, read the text below. Use the word given in capitals at the end of some of the lines to form a word that fits in the gap **in the same line**. There is an example at the beginning (**0**).

Example: 0 EMPLOYEES

The push that made a career change happen

Many **(0)** .... who have had one job for a while may dream about doing something different.	EMPLOY
However, few make the dream a **(1)** .... because the thought of having to start from the	REAL
beginning again can be too **(2)**	TERRIFY
Occasionally, though, a helpful push in a new direction occurs **(3)** .... This happened to Alex, who was working in a coffee shop.	EXPECTED
Lucy works for an **(4)** .... agency near the coffee shop, and she goes there for breakfast. She	EMPLOY
noticed that Alex had **(5)** .... customer service skills. Alex was always smiling, helpful and	IMPRESS
never got orders wrong. So when a **(6)**	VACANT
for a customer services position came up in a telecommunications company that her agency represents, Lucy thought of Alex.	
Lucy spoke to her manager, who agreed to ask Alex to apply. Alex was ready for a career change, so, with	
Lucy's **(7)** .... and advice, he accepted the challenge. He joined the company as a	ENCOURAGE
(8) .... on a six month contract, but was	TRAIN
offered a permanent position after just two months.	

Listening

Part 2

1 Look at the exam task instructions.

1 What is Leila's job?

2 How long should your answers be?

2 Look at the exam task questions 1–10 and think of some words that could fit in each gap.

3 🔊 **05** Now listen and do the exam task.

Need help? Go to Quick steps page 41 in the Student's Book

✓ Exam task

You will hear a woman called Leila Osman talking on a podcast about working as a bike courier in London. For questions **1–10**, complete the sentences with a word or short phrase.

Leila says the best thing about her job is the **(1)** .... it gives her.

Leila works for a company which provides her with a **(2)** .... to use at work.

Leila admits the **(3)** .... that she bought for work cost her a lot of money.

Leila's **(4)** .... taught her to repair tyres.

Leila says in large, modern buildings, she usually collects items from the **(5)** ....

When Leila tells the courier company that she is **(6)** ...., she means she is ready to take more jobs from them.

When Leila chats with other couriers about the job, one thing they complain about is their **(7)** ....

Leila usually works for **(8)** .... hours a day.

Leila says she found it hard to build her **(9)** .... in riding a bike in the city.

Leila would like to become a **(10)** .... in the future.

Writing

1 Look at the exam task and answer these questions.

1 What is the job and how long is it for?
2 Why is it helpful to speak English in this job?
3 What three questions must you answer in your letter?
4 How will this letter be different from an email to a good friend?

✓ Exam task

You have seen this job advertisement in an English-language newspaper.

Photographer's assistant wanted

A fun job helping a photographer take pictures at large summer weddings for couples from around the world

for the summer only

Please write to the photographer, Mr Robert Kelly, saying

• when you will be able to start work
• how well you can speak English and any other languages
• why you are interested in doing this job

Write your **letter of application** in **140–190** words in an appropriate style.

2 Read the model letter and find where each of the following is mentioned. Write the correct line number or numbers next to each one.

		Line number(s)
1	what he has sent with the letter	....
2	answer to bullet point 3	....
3	where he found out about the job	....
4	his relevant experience	....
5	answer to bullet point 1	....
6	answer to bullet point 2	....
7	a reason for writing	....

Dear <u>Rob</u>,

I am writing in response to your advertisment in the newspaper for a photographer's assisstant. I <u>want</u> to apply
5 for the job.

I am currently a student at Hillview College, studying photography and art. I am very keen to gain some experience with a proffessional photographer, as it is my
10 ambition to be one in the future. Because I have studied photography, I <u>reckon</u> I have <u>tons of</u> skills that would be useful in this job.

I will also be able to help you give
15 instructions to wedding guests about where they should stand, <u>etc</u>. because I speak several languages. I have reached intamediate level in both English and French, and elementry level with Chinese.
20 My native language is Spanish.

My term finishes at the end of May, and after that time, <u>I'll</u> be able to work any day and time you want. Before that, I would be <u>OK</u> to work in the evenings and at weekends.
25 I enclose my CV, and I look forward to hearing from you.

<u>Best wishes</u>,

Emilio Juan

3 Change the underlined words in the model letter to more appropriate ones.

4 Find and correct five spelling mistakes in the model letter.

5 Plan and write your letter. Follow the instructions in the exam task.

Need help? Go to Quick steps page 45 and the Writing bank page 120 in the Student's Book

Listening

Part 1

1 Look at questions 1–4 in the exam task. Statements 1–6 below are false, explain why.

1 Questions 1–4 all involve the same speakers.
2 In Question 1, the running coach is complaining about some runners.
3 In Question 2, the mother has a headache.
4 Question 3 focuses on the man's opinion.
5 Question 4 focuses on a detail mentioned by the woman.
6 This exam task is exactly the same as Part 1 in the exam.

2 🔊 **06** Now listen and do the exam task.

Need help? Go to Quick steps page 48 in the Student's Book

✓ Exam task

You will hear people talking in four different situations (in the exam you will hear eight). For questions **1–4**, choose the best answer (**A**, **B** or **C**).

1 You hear a running coach giving advice about the week before a marathon.
    What kind of advice does she give?
    A how to maintain the right level of physical fitness
    B how to assess any injuries that may occur
    C how to deal with an issue mentally

2 You hear a woman phoning her daughter about an arrangement for tonight.
    What does the woman say about her back problem?
    A She has tried to treat it without success.
    B She wants to stop it becoming more serious.
    C She thinks it is worse now than it has been before.

3 You hear a man talking about a change in his diet.
    He says one effect of the diet is that
    A he realises how unhealthy he is.
    B he is able to achieve more.
    C he lacks energy at times.

4 You hear a woman giving advice to footballers about looking after their feet.
    What advice does she give them?
    A Check your feet and boots after playing.
    B Get yourself the right boots.
    C Treat any foot injuries immediately.

Grammar
Relative clauses

1 💿 Some of these sentences written by exam candidates contain mistakes. Correct any mistakes and/or add any missing commas. Tick the sentences that are correct.

1 That's the house where we used to live in when I was a child.
2 The athlete which won a gold medal four years ago only managed 10th place this year.
3 Nobody wants to sit at the table where is nearest to the door – it's too cold.
4 Leo's favourite programmes are documentaries which is surprising for a ten-year-old.
5 The doctor, who I've never been to before, gave me some very effective tablets.
6 Do you know who's phone this is? I just found it on the floor.
7 In October, when I start university, my mum's renting my room to a lodger.
8 I'm lucky to have a piano teacher whose flat is in the same block as mine.
9 My hair was cut by Ricardo who went to school with me.
10 I visited the town which my mum grew up last summer.

2 Complete these sentences with suitable relative pronouns. Add commas where necessary. In some cases, more than one answer is possible. Which of the relative pronouns in 1–6 could we leave out?

1 The tennis club .... I learnt to play is shutting down soon.

2 My neighbour .... I've known since I was very young has just won a medal at the Olympics.

3 Why don't you want this fish .... I've just cooked for you? It's really healthy!

4 I think the university's new facilities will be great for students .... are studying sport.

5 Tom plays handball .... he learnt to play at school in the local league.

6 Roger Federer is a tennis player .... achievements will be hard to beat.

Vocabulary

1 Replace the underlined words with phrasal verbs formed by adding *up* to the correct form of these verbs.

> dress   heal   speed   stay   use   tidy

1 I don't like wearing special clothes .... when I go out. It makes me feel uncomfortable.

2 If you're serious about being an elite runner, you have to stop going to bed .... so late.

3 The nasty cut on my finger took a long time to get better ....

4 Before we cook dinner, we need to clear away .... all the mess my little brother made earlier.

5 I've finished .... all the sun cream we had – can you get some more when you go shopping?

6 If the driver in second place doesn't go faster .... now, he's going to lose the race.

2 Use the clues to complete the crossword. Then write a word using the letters in the shaded boxes.

Across

1 A doctor gives you a … for tablets or medicines.

5 There is growing recognition that a person's … health affects their physical health.

7 Listening to calming music can have a … effect.

9 If you have an eye …, it can affect your ability to see.

10 If a bone is broken in more than one place, it can take a long time to … .

Down

2 When you get ill, you hope for a quick … .

3 Health … systems vary a lot from country to country.

4 If you have a very high …, you feel hot and unwell.

6 When you have a deep or large cut, you may need a nurse to give you some … .

8 Drinking herbal tea can … headaches.

Letters from the shaded boxes make the word:

....

Reading and Use of English

Need help? Go to Quick steps Part 2 page 52 in the Student's Book

✓ Exam task

For questions **1–8**, read the text below and think of the word which best fits each gap.
Use only **one** word in each gap. There is an example at the beginning (**0**).

Example: 0 ONE

Angela Eiter: rock superstar!

Angela ('Angy') Eiter from Austria is **(0)** .... of the best female rock climbers in the world. The **(1)** .... outstanding thing she achieved in competitive climbing was winning the World Championships, **(2)** .... she won for the first time in 2004, and three more times after that.

In **(3)** .... to her competition wins, Angy has climbed many of the world's hardest routes on rock. In 2017, after overcoming a serious shoulder injury, Eiter reached the peak **(4)** .... her climbing career, when she climbed a route called La Planta di Shiva in Spain. Only two other people, both men, have ever managed **(5)** .... climb anything more difficult.

Angela **(6)** .... longer climbs competitively, but she still climbs professionally all around the world. She says it's not the difficulty of climbs that's important. **(7)** .... matters to her is developing her ability to climb in a wider variety of contexts. Eiter also coaches young athletes to push themselves to their limits, just **(8)** .... she has done herself.

Writing

Part 2 letter

1 Look at the exam task and answer these questions.

1 Who is Toni?
2 How many questions does Toni ask in the letter?
3 How do you know this is an informal letter?
4 How many words must you write?

✓ Exam task

Here is part of a letter you have received from an English-speaking friend, Toni.

> At the moment, I'm trying to improve my diet by eating more fruit and vegetables. I'm finding it really hard because I prefer chocolate and cakes! Do you always try to eat healthily? What sort of food do you eat? And what else do you do to keep fit and healthy? Write back soon!
> All the best,
> Toni

Write your **letter** in **140–190** words in an appropriate style.

2 Read the model letter and answer the following questions.

1 Which paragraph answers Toni's first question?
2 Which paragraph answers Toni's third question?
3 What does Mick do in the first paragraph?
4 What other opening and closing formulas could Mick use in this letter to his friend?

3 Write a suitable purpose link in the two gaps in the text.

4 Plan and write your letter. Follow the instructions in the exam task.

Need help? Go to Quick steps page 53 and the Writing bank page 120 in the Student's Book

Opening formula

Hi Toni,

1 It was great to get your letter and to hear about what you're doing at the moment. Well done for trying to improve your diet. I agree eating healthily isn't easy – I love chocolate and cakes too!

2 In answer to your first question, I'd say my diet's generally quite healthy. My dad insists I eat dinner with him every evening .... he can make sure I eat plenty of vegetables and fruit. And although I like sweet things, I only have them occasionally. I have to admit though, that when I'm at college, I often have a burger and fries for lunch. I know they're not good for me but I can't resist them!

3 You also asked me about what else I do to stay fit and healthy. One thing I do is a lot of walking – I have to, as I haven't got my driving licence yet. I walk to college and to friends' houses nearby. I also go to bed quite early ....to get plenty of sleep. That's a nice, easy way to stay healthy!

Looking forward to hearing from you soon.

Closing formula

All the best,

Mick

Feeling the heat

Reading and Use of English

Part 6

1 Read the exam task instructions. Answer these questions.

1 What building material is the article about?

2 How many extra sentences are there?

2 Now do the exam task. Use the words underlined in the text to help you choose the right answer.

Need help? Go to Quick steps page 54 in the Student's Book

✓ Exam task

You are going to read an article about building with bamboo. Six sentences have been removed from the article. Choose from the sentences **A–G** the one which fits each gap (**1–6**). There is one extra sentence which you do not need to use.

A Rather than tiles or slates, this is covered in thousands of little plants.

B These forms were bent into shape through a fire baking process.

C The 1,600-square-metre structure is made entirely of this natural material.

D The massive bamboo pavilion was designed to reflect this theme.

E Instead of being thrown into land-fill like conventional building waste, bamboo will biodegrade.

F One of the reasons for its enduring appeal is its remarkable strength.

G For example, without treatment to protect bamboo from insects and the weather, it doesn't have the lifespan of concrete.

Bamboo: a building material of the past and for the future

Of all the substances humans use, only water is used in larger amounts than concrete. Concrete, which is made from cement, water and stone, is an incredibly valuable construction material. However, cement manufacturing releases high levels of CO_2, concrete mixing requires huge quantities of water, and concrete buildings absorb the sun's heat, making urban areas hotter. Consequently, many engineers and building designers are trying to find alternative construction materials.

For thousands of years, bamboo has been used as a building material across Asia and South America, where it grows easily and abundantly. Today, there are over six million hectares of this plant being grown in China, and ten million people are employed in industries relating to bamboo cultivation and use. **1** Bamboo can tolerate greater tension than mild steel, and can stand twice as much pressure as concrete.

Now that there is a need for more sustainable building methods to combat global warming, modern architects from around the world are turning to bamboo as an alternative to steel and concrete. In 2019, Italian architect Mauricio Cardenas Laverde completed one of the largest bamboo projects in China, the Bamboo Eye pavilion, an outstanding example of what can be done with it. **2** Not only does <u>this mean</u> that the building required no concrete or steel in its construction, but the 5,000 poles required to build it were harvested locally from a bamboo forest, so transportation demands were kept to a minimum.

The Bamboo Eye pavilion resembles a long, low, smooth hill. Its rounded outline is created with bamboo arches, which are nine metres high, and span a width of 32 metres. **3** As well as turning the bamboo from green to a golden yellow, <u>this treatment</u> helps to extend its life.

Being made of moso bamboo, a type that has the shape of a round tube, the frame that holds the pavilion up is relatively lightweight: another advantage of this amazing material, which makes it easier to move and work with than materials like concrete. Yet <u>this structure</u> is also strong enough to bear the weight of a green roof. **4** As well as being a more sustainable roofing method, <u>this also helps</u> the pavilion blend in with the countryside that surrounds it.

The Bamboo Eye was built to house the International Horticultural Exhibition in Beijing, a six-month show attracting visitors from all over the world to see show gardens and flower displays. The exhibition emphasises how to live closer to nature in a more <u>sustainable</u> way, with as little damage to the environment as possible. **5** It does so by showcasing the architectural possibilities of bamboo in low-carbon construction.

Indeed, Laverde hopes his bamboo pavilion proves to people all over the world that bamboo is a construction material of the future. Of course, bamboo does have disadvantages, which have to be overcome when used in building. **6** However, as long as a structure made from bamboo is looked after properly, it can last hundreds of years. And after that, it can be easily and cheaply replaced with another structure made from bamboo – the ultimate renewable material.

Vocabulary

Collocations

Match these words to form collocations about environmental issues.

1	industrial	a	icecaps
2	acid	b	change
3	carbon	c	farming
4	melting	d	spill
5	fossil	e	rain
6	solar	f	gases
7	oil	g	waste
8	climate	h	fuels
9	global	i	footprint
10	greenhouse	j	diet
11	intensive	k	power
12	plant-based	l	warming

Listening

Part 3

 Read the exam task instructions and answer these questions.

1 What is the topic of the five monologues?
2 How many of the options A–H won't you need to use?
3 What do you think you should do before you listen to Speaker 1?

2 🔊 **07** Now listen and do the exam task.

Need help? Go to Quick steps page 57 in the Student's Book

✓ Exam task

You will hear five short extracts in which people are giving advice about taking a more sustainable approach to clothes. For questions **1–5**, choose from the list (**A–H**) what advice each speaker gives. Use the letters only once. There are three extra letters which you do not need to use.

A Transform items you already own.
B Repair damaged items rather than replacing them.
C Buy things for long-term use.
D Do not buy items made from certain fabrics.
E Buy good quality second-hand clothes.
F Do not follow the latest fashions too closely.
G Plan your clothes purchases carefully.
H Do not let people's reactions to your efforts stop you.

Speaker 1	1
Speaker 2	2
Speaker 3	3
Speaker 4	4
Speaker 5	5

Grammar

a b c

Conditionals 1–3, mixed conditionals

◎ Some of these sentences written by exam candidates contain mistakes. Correct any mistakes.

1 Jean Paul would be more likely to get a job if he would have some qualifications.
2 If I were you, I wouldn't sell your bike, because you might need it one day.
3 If Diana hadn't give me a lift, I wouldn't be here so early.
4 If her friend hadn't encouraged her, she won't have bought such an expensive suit.
5 The party will be a disaster unless we get a DJ booked soon.
6 If the flat had been further out of the city, they wouldn't have bought it.
7 If Holly had worked harder, she wouldn't have been unemployed now.
8 Would so many people want to go to the restaurant if it hadn't been on the TV?
9 Jimmy would have crashed into the deer if it didn't run off the road just in time.
10 If they hadn't closed the sports centre, people in this town wouldn't be so unfit now.

Reading and Use of English

Part 4

1 Read the exam instructions.

1 What must not be changed when you write your answer?
2 What must be the same in the first and second sentences?
3 Should you write just one word for your answer?

2 Read the example. How do you know you need to write a clause with *if*?

3 Now do the exam task.

Need help? Go to Quick steps page 60 in the Student's Book

For questions **1–6**, complete the second sentence so that it has a similar meaning to the first sentence, using the word given. **Do not change the word given**. You must use between **two** and **five** words, including the word given. Here is an example (**0**).

Example:

0 It rained heavily, which caused the river to rise.
RISEN
The river
WOULD NOT / WOULDN'T HAVE RISEN IF it hadn't rained heavily.

1 It was only because Harry helped us that we managed to get the wardrobe upstairs.
ABLE
If Harry hadn't helped us, we
.... to get the wardrobe upstairs.

2 Most of the town's population is happy for more trees to be planted in the centre.
FAVOUR
Most residents of the town
.... more trees being planted in the centre.

3 Children can't go into the wildlife park while work to build the new pond continues.
PROGRESS
While building work on the new pond
...., children are not allowed into the wildlife park.

4 Despite getting many warnings from scientists about global warming, governments have done little to stop it.
EVEN
Governments have done little to stop global warming ....
given them many warnings about it.

5 You shouldn't get a job in conservation unless you're really passionate about it.
IF
You should get a job in conservation only
.... deal of passion for it.

6 The increased use of traditional farming methods might bring wildlife back to the countryside.
USED
If traditional farming methods
.... often, wildlife might return to the countryside.

Writing

1 Look at the exam task and answer these questions.

1 How many words is the minimum you should write?
2 What is the topic of the essay?
3 Do you agree with the statement?
4 Should you write about what you think?

✅ Exam task

You have had a class discussion on the harm plastic waste does to the environment. Now, your teacher has asked you to write an essay. Write an essay using all the notes and give reasons for your point of view.

All plastic packaging should be banned.
Do you agree?

Notes
Write about:
1 keeping food fresh
2 plastic in the oceans
3 your own idea

Write your **essay** in **140–190** words. You must use grammatically correct sentences with accurate spelling and punctuation in an appropriate style.

2 Look at the four words in bold that begin sentences in the essay. What do they signal?

1 .... means you should expect a contrast within the sentence.
2 .... means you should expect a contrast with the previous sentence.
3 .... means you should expect a reason in the sentence.
4 .... means you should expect a result in the sentence.

3 Plan and write your essay. Follow the instructions in the exam task.

Need help? Go to Quick steps page 61 and the Writing bank page 118 in the Student's Book

Recently, there has been a lot of discussion in the media about the impact of plastic rubbish on the environment. Plastic, a material made from oil, creates a particularly bad waste problem because it cannot be broken down by natural means. **Consequently**, it stays with us forever.

Business sectors such as the food and drinks industry rely heavily on various types of plastic. **Because** it is strong, waterproof and flexible, plastic is the ideal packaging material for keeping products fresh and undamaged during transportation and when they are on sale in shops.

However, although some of this plastic packaging can be recycled, it all eventually gets dumped in landfill, where it pollutes the ground. A huge amount also ends up in the ocean, where it poisons fish and other sea animals. Conservationists say they have found plastic in every part of every ocean.

To prevent this problem from getting even worse, we need to find new ways to package products. Nowadays, there are some good alternatives to plastic. **While** they have the same properties as plastic, they will biodegrade over time. If we want to save our oceans we need to stop using oil-based plastic.

Reading and Use of English

Part 5

1 Read the exam task instructions and the title. Answer these questions.

1 What is the writer worried about?

2 What do you expect a scientist to say about this topic?

2 Now do the exam task.

Need help? Go to Quick steps page 62 in the Student's Book

Getting facts from the internet: does it ruin your memory?

Do you ever use an encyclopaedia? It's unlikely that anyone nowadays will answer 'yes' to this question, since internet search engines have made them almost completely redundant as a means of finding out about the world. If you want to educate yourself about anything from when steam engines were invented to what an aardvark is, you ask the internet. But once you have the answers (1698 and an African mammal), do you remember these facts? And does it matter if you don't? After all, you can always just ask the internet again.

Because it's my birthday soon, the aging process has been on my mind recently, and I've become very aware of how often I reach for my phone to find a fact that I know but cannot recall: that film star's name, the year the Russians first went into space, and so on. This has made me start to wonder if I rely on the internet too much. Perhaps the saying 'use it or lose it' applies to memory. While getting facts from the internet is wonderfully easy and immediate, is it making my brain lazy?

I researched the topic (online of course). One interesting, and rather surprising, search result was the work of Dr Richard Carmona, a scientist from the U.S. He says it's certainly true that many people feel they can't live without their phones, a feeling that's sometimes as strong as an addiction. However, he says there's no clear evidence to suggest that reliance on the internet as a back-up memory leads to a lazy brain. In fact, he claims that the brain stays more engaged because you're providing it with so much information to process. Over time, this constant input creates more networks in the brain and they actually aid our memory.

To find out for myself, yesterday I decided not to use my phone when I couldn't recall something. I wanted to see

if my own recall improved when I stopped relying on the internet. At first, it was fine. Then a friend asked if I knew who'd directed a film. The director's name was in my memory, but it was escaping me. I fought the desire to pick up my phone, and tried to force the name into my mind. It didn't work, and I ended up feeling stressed and frustrated. Dr Carmona says these feelings are often the cost of not taking the easy internet option. I also felt I'd wasted ages trying to remember something when a search engine could have found it in seconds. While brushing my teeth before bed, I finally remembered the director's name.

So why did it take me so long to remember? Dr Carmona says that memories are saved like a series of files but some essential information like our addresses, are remembered as more important than others. These remain easier to access in the memory, as if they were on top of a stack of *line 50* files. Less significant information gets stashed away at the bottom of the stack – still there, but harder to recall. If I try to remember an unimportant detail like a film director's name, I have to go a long way down the memory stack to find it. Being unable to recall it doesn't mean my brain's getting lazy.

Listening to Dr Carmona, it seems I can stop worrying, and forget about using a printed encyclopaedia rather than an electronic search engine to improve my brain power. However, one thing I did enjoy when I was doing without internet searches was the joy I felt when I managed to recall something using brain power. I might have the occasional internet-free day just so I can experience a few more of those moments. And as more birthdays pass, I ought perhaps to take Dr Carmona's advice on other ways of keeping the brain healthy, such as sleeping well, and getting enough exercise.

You are going to read an article about relying on the internet and the effect of that on memory. For questions **1–6**, choose the answer (**A**, **B**, **C** or **D**) which you think fits best according to the text.

1 In the first paragraph, what does the writer say about encyclopaedias?
   A They were an effective means of learning.
   B They contained an incredibly broad range of information.
   C They can still help people memorise facts.
   D They have lost their usefulness.

2 What has the writer noticed recently?
   A the value of expanding her memory in certain areas
   B the need to start working on maintaining a good memory
   C the frequency of gaps in her memory
   D the importance of trusting her own memory

3 Dr Carmona says that getting information from the internet
   A keeps the brain stimulated.
   B weakens your long-term memory.
   C increases dependence on phones.
   D improves the ability to select relevant information.

4 In the fourth paragraph, the writer explains
   A one reason she disagrees with Dr Carmona.
   B how changing a habit was surprisingly simple.
   C the advantages of relying on your memory alone.
   D how she struggled with an experiment.

5 What does *stashed away* mean in line 50?
   A displayed before use
   B kept in a favourable position
   C lost and never found
   D stored in a hidden place

6 In the final paragraph, the writer says she has found out that
   A it would be difficult to follow all Dr Carmona's recommendations.
   B the experience of keeping off the internet is worth repeating.
   C finding information in print is hard work but can be fun.
   D it is not necessary to do anything differently because of her age.

Grammar

a   b

Articles

1 ⊙ **Some of these sentences written by exam candidates contain mistakes. Correct any mistakes, using *a*, *the* or no article.**

1 My wife's family is from United States, and that's where we met.
2 When I'm on holiday at the beach, I have swim every morning.
3 When you cross this road, be very careful because of all the cars that speed down here.
4 I don't think Laura's uncle is very nice person.
5 Take fewer, shorter showers to save the energy.
6 I like playing handball most as it's a very exciting game.
7 There's an article here about how most children want to help protect an environment.
8 At the moment, I am student at university but I'm in my final year.
9 We're planning to watch a documentary this evening on civilisation of ancient Ethiopia.
10 Like all the inventions, the computer has brought about unexpected developments.

Passive forms

2 **Put the words and phrases in the correct order to form passive sentences.**

1 taken / the photos / photographer / a professional / were / by
2 want / be / a new hall / the students / whether / should / they / asked
3 yet / fixed / speakers / been / have / your / ?
4 to / recorded / be / most music / tape / onto / used
5 thought / to / are / be / falling / pollution levels
6 been / the terms of the agreement / both sides / agreed / have / by / not yet
7 expected / the new president / Sarah James / be / is / to
8 be / by / the new theatre / constructed / a local company / will
9 known / whether / not / the disease / it / cure / the new drug / is / will
10 are / to / escaped / a moped / the thieves / on / thought / have

Reading and Use of English

Part 1

1 Look at the exam task example. How do we know the correct answer is *wastes*?

A It is the only grammatically correct answer.

B It collocates with *time* in the text after the gap.

2 Quickly read the text. Is this a factual text or an opinion-based one?

3 Now do the exam task.

Need help? Go to Quick steps page 67 in the Student's Book

✓ Exam task

For questions **1–8**, read the text below and decide which answer (**A**, **B**, **C** or **D**) best fits each gap. There is an example at the beginning (**0**).

Example: 0   **A** deletes   **B** wastes   **C** removes   **D** misses

How social media helps me

Social media is often discussed in terms of the harm it causes: it **(0)** ....B......... a great deal of time, it encourages you to be vain, it allows people to **(1)** .... negative ideas around the world. **(2)** ...., young people are often advised to spend time offline every day.

However, we shouldn't overlook the ways in which social media can enrich people's lives. As a student, social media provides me with a very **(3)** .... break from essay-writing or reading academic texts. Spending ten minutes **(4)** .... through messages and comments takes my mind off work. It can also **(5)** .... me with new ideas, and after a long day of lectures or exams, I use social media as a wonderful **(6)** .... art gallery. Looking at the beautiful or amusing images people have posted really **(7)** .... me up.

We shouldn't think of social media purely as a menace to society. How good or bad it is simply **(8)** .... on the way it is used.

1	**A** drive	**B** spread	**C** extend	**D** cover
2	**A** Alternatively	**B** Consequently	**C** Similarly	**D** Admittedly
3	**A** welcome	**B** comfortable	**C** acceptable	**D** required
4	**A** entering	**B** typing	**C** scrolling	**D** shifting
5	**A** persuade	**B** convince	**C** impact	**D** inspire
6	**A** technical	**B** mechanical	**C** virtual	**D** electrical
7	**A** cheers	**B** fills	**C** catches	**D** raises
8	**A** effects	**B** depends	**C** relies	**D** applies

Listening

Part 2

1 Make sure you know the meaning of virtual reality (VR). What can VR be used for?

2 Read the exam task instructions. Who will you hear speaking? What will this person be talking about?

3 Read through the questions and think about what kind of word might go in each gap.

4 🔊 **08** Now listen and do the exam task.

Need help? Go to Quick steps page 64 in the Student's Book

✓ Exam task

You will hear a woman called Marta talking about a technology museum. For questions **1–10**, complete the sentences with a word or short phrase.

The technology museum is designed to look like a **(1)** ....

After being redesigned, the museum opened again in **(2)** ....

You can reserve a place on the tour of the museum a maximum of **(3)** .... before your visit.

In the part of the museum called the Present Zone, Marta went **(4)** .... using virtual reality technology.

In the Future Zone, Marta particularly enjoyed the room featuring the future of **(5)** ....

Marta's first mission was to plan a **(6)** .... of some people who had been caught in a wildfire.

In the medical room, Marta learnt about future technology being able to predict the **(7)** .... that people will have.

On the tour, Marta's group saw how **(8)** .... might meet in the future.

In the 'Teleport Room', a virtual reality device made Marta appear to have the arms of a **(9)** ....

Marta was told that a museum visitor who was a **(10)** .... wanted a home containing the same technology as the museum.

Writing

Part 2 article

1 Look at the exam task and answer these questions.

1 Who are you writing an article for?
2 What will happen if you write a very good article?
3 What do you have to write about?

✓ Exam task

You have seen this announcement in an English-language magazine called *Click!*

We'd like to publish readers' most interesting articles about:

CHOOSING NOT TO USE TECHNOLOGY

Write about something you do instead of using technology and say:
- why you prefer not to use the technology available
- whether you will continue with this habit.

Write your **article** in **140–190** words.

2 Read the model article and answer these questions.

1 Look at the four numbered words in bold. <u>Underline</u> the words below which could correctly replace them.

1 Although	However	Because
2 so	though	therefore
3 On account of	Consequently	Even though
4 since	despite	so

2 Find one sentence that has a passive verb form.
3 Which phrases make the article sound lively?

3 Plan and write your article. Follow the instructions in the exam task.

Need help? Go to Quick steps page 69 and the Writing bank page 124 in the Student's Book

Choosing not to use technology

In general, I have no problem with technology. I use a mobile phone and I have a virtual assistant at home. **Since**[1] I work as a trainee accountant, I also use a PC all day. However, one thing I'm not so keen on using technology for is reading newspapers. I could easily read my paper online, **but**[2] I prefer not to.

The main reason for this is my morning routine. I always stop for a coffee on my way to work at a café where newspapers are supplied for customers. So while I'm sipping my cappuccino, I read the news. I like holding the newspaper, looking through it, and choosing something to read.

I've tried the mobile version, but it's not nearly as good. To get through an article online, you have to scroll up and down a lot. As a **result**[3], I find it difficult to focus on what I'm reading. Furthermore, **as**[4] I look at a screen all day, I believe it's better for my eyes to keep off my phone. So I definitely won't be changing this habit any time soon!

Breaking news

Reading and Use of English

Part 4

Do the exam task

Need help? Go to Quick steps page 83 in the Student's book

✓ Exam task

For questions **1–6**, complete the second sentence so that it has a similar meaning to the first sentence, using the word given. **Do not change the word given.** You must use between **two** and **five** words, including the word given. Here is an example (**0**).

Example (0): 'Can I sit next to you, Katie?' said Charlotte.
WHETHER
Charlotte asked ...WHETHER SHE COULD SIT... next to Katie.

1 'Hiking is very challenging on the mountain in winter,' the guide told us.
   WARNED
   The guide .... very challenging on the mountain in winter.

2 'Do you know anything about producing videos?' Pippa asked me.
   IF
   Pippa asked me ....
   anything about producing videos.

3 Social media influencers have to research products before they promote them.
   MUST
   Products that social media influencers promote .... by them first.

4 The next series of *Wilderland* can be streamed from March 19th.
   POSSIBLE
   It will .... the next series of *Wilderland* from March 19th.

5 Laura is arranging the catering for the film crew.
   ARRANGEMENTS
   Laura is .... the catering for the film crew.

6 'I'm not telling you what your present is – it's a surprise!' Ben told Eve.
   REFUSED
   Ben .... Eve what her present was – it was a surprise.

Vocabulary

Noun suffixes

1 Complete the crossword with nouns formed from these words. 'pl' means the noun is plural. Be careful with 2 and 8 – make sure you choose the noun that fits in the spaces.

Across
2 vary
5 arrange (pl)
7 prefer (pl)
8 identify (pl)
9 contribute
10 coincide

Down
1 less
3 freeze
4 introduce
6 appear

2 Complete the sentences using a form of the word in brackets. Use prefixes and suffixes or make internal spelling changes.

1 In our team, the various.................... (able) of staff members are all very useful.

2 The journalist said she had definite .... (prove) of the murderer's identity.

3 The .... (die) of the film star was announced by his family yesterday.

4 I'm not going to watch that series because all its .... (view) are so bad.

5 The film's great except for its .... (long) – I thought it would never end!

6 The actor managed to show us the .... (deep) of the character's feelings brilliantly.

7 Everyone has great .... (admire) for the way Mike dealt with his problems.

8 Much to my brother's .... (amuse), I fell over while I was running to my car!

9 Sorry if you feel embarrassed – that was not my .... (intend)!

10 There has recently been a dramatic .... (reduce) in the number of cars entering the city.

Reading and Use of English

1 Look at the exam text gaps and the words on the right. Answer these questions.

1 All the answers are nouns. Which gap must be filled with a plural noun?

2 Which nouns will be made with a suffix or a prefix, and which will require changes within the given word?

2 Now do the exam task.

Need help? Go to Quick steps page 76 in the Student's Book

✓ Exam task

For questions **1–8**, read the text below. Use the word given in capitals at the end of some of the lines to form a word that fits in the gap **in the same line**. There is an example at the beginning (**0**).

Example: 0 BEAUTY

Why social media stars have more cultural influence than other celebrities

Social media stars are now a more powerful influence on culture, fashion and **(0)** .... than traditional celebrities such as film and TV stars. Although the **(1)** .... of traditional celebrities have a social media profile, this does not give them the **(2)** .... with their followers that social media stars have.

BEAUTIFUL

MAJOR

CONNECT

Social media stars, or 'influencers', develop online groups of followers and build high levels of **(3)** .... in them. Influencers establish these successful **(4)** .... with their followers mainly by being constantly available for comment and frequently posting new **(5)** .... on their accounts. Furthermore, some traditional celebrities have such a strong **(6)** .... for using social media that they hire someone else to run their accounts. Comments on these from fans often fail to get any **(7)** .... at all.

COMMIT

RELATION

CONTAIN

LIKE

RESPOND

Another key thing that explains the success of social media stars is that they rise to celebrity status through direct, personal interaction with their fans. Traditional celebrities can become stars with very little direct **(8)** .... with their audience.

INVOLVE

Listening

Part 4

1 Look at the exam task instructions and answer these questions.

1 Who will you hear and what will he be talking about?

2 *AI* stands for *advanced information / artificial intelligence*

2 Underline the key words in the first line of each question.

3 🔊 **09** Now listen and do the exam task.

Need help? Go to Quick steps page 72 in the Student's Book

✓ Exam task

You will hear a radio interview with a media expert called Dr Khalid Ali, who talks about the use of artificial intelligence in journalism. For questions **1–7**, choose the best answer (**A**, **B** or **C**).

1 Why did Dr Ali want to appear on the programme?
A to prepare people for the future of journalism
B to help people appreciate the importance of journalism
C to make people aware of the current situation in journalism

2 What does Dr Ali say about using AI to collect data for journalism?
A The news industry is ahead of other businesses.
B There is nothing unique about such a strategy.
C The amount of data involved is hard to manage.

3 Dr Ali thinks that the use of AI to identify fake news
A may fail on some online platforms.
B requires people to be involved.
C will soon become unnecessary.

4 Dr Ali says that using AI to monitor comments on articles will lead to
A more articles offering readers the opportunity to comment.
B fewer offensive comments being left by readers.
C more readers being able to comment on each article.

5 What does Dr Ali think is the main advantage of graphics produced by AI?
A They are much clearer.
B They are more attractive.
C They are more complex.

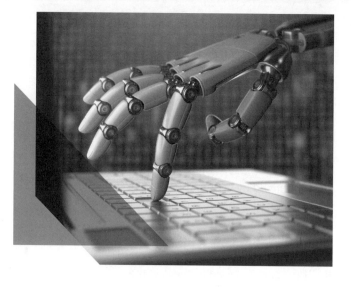

6 Dr Ali thinks that in the news industry, interactive tools such as 'chat media' will
A quickly become more popular.
B usually be added to articles as a fun extra.
C only be used in certain countries.

7 What does Dr Ali say about the future of journalists?
A Their roles will expand.
B Computers will do most of their work.
C They will be able to avoid boring tasks.

Grammar

Reported speech and reporting verbs

⊙ **Correct the reported speech and reporting verb mistakes in these sentences written by exam candidates. One sentence has two errors.**

1 My boss said she looked at my report tomorrow morning.
2 I asked the baker whether she have any fresh croissants that morning.
3 George wanted to pay the bill but I insisted on pay half.
4 Christina had forgotten to get a present for her dad but she told her mum she bought him something.
5 Yesterday evening, I decided that I will get a job rather than go to university.
6 In last week's episode of the thriller, the journalist threatened of exposing the president's lies.
7 We asked the teacher what was happened and he said that a student broke the window accidentally.
8 Our uncle invited us for go on holiday on his yacht.
9 I watched the news at nine o'clock and it said that Leonardo Mario won the election.
10 My friend reminded me do not to turn on your phone in the hospital.

Writing

1 Look at the exam task and answer these questions.

1 Who is coming to the college?
2 What is she going to do?
3 What three things must you write about?
4 What is the minimum number of words you should write?
5 What would be the most suitable style to write in?

✓ Exam task

A famous journalist has been invited to come and give a talk to students at your college. Your teacher has asked you to write a report about:

- what information you would like her to give in her talk
- how long the talk should be
- what follow-up activities students could do in class afterwards

Write your **report** in **140–190** words.

2 Read the model report and complete it with the following phrases.

> After the talk   Alternatively
> It would be interesting   It would be sensible
> The aim   To sum up

3 Plan and write your report. Follow the instructions in the exam task.

Need help? Go to Quick steps page 77 and the Writing bank page 126 in the Student's Book

---

The journalist's talk

Introduction

(1) .... of this report is to put forward suggestions for the content and length of the talk, and some possible follow-up activities for students to do in class afterwards.

Content of the talk

(2) .... to hear about some of the journalist's most exciting experiences in her job. Also, in view of the fact that the audience will be made up principally of students who are considering their future careers, it would be useful to hear about the best way to become a journalist, and whether she would recommend it.

Length of the talk

(3) .... to ask her to talk for 50 minutes, the length of a college lesson, in order that it will fit in with the college timetable.

Follow-up activities

(4) .... , students could research articles written by the journalist, and choose one to write a review of.

(5) .... , students could write an article themselves.

Conclusion

(6) .... , the journalist would ideally give a talk of 50 minutes about exciting experiences she has had and how to become a journalist. Afterwards, students could write an article or a review of one.

10 Shopping around

Listening

Part 3

1 Look at the exam task instructions. What are the five people talking about? Think of some ways you could do this and note down the key vocabulary.

2 Read answer options A–H. Write down a word or phrase that means the same as each underlined part of A–H.

3 🔊 **10** Now listen and do the exam task.

Need help? Go to Quick steps page 80 in the Student's Book

✓ Exam task

You will hear five short extracts in which people are talking about how they have reduced the number of things they buy. For questions **1–5**, choose from the list (**A–H**) how each person has reduced the number of things they buy. Use the letters only once. There are three extra letters which you do not need to use.

A I <u>delay</u> making purchases.
B I choose something <u>to save money for</u>.
C I identify what is <u>motivating me</u> to buy something.
D I <u>give away</u> money instead of buying things for myself.
E I pay with cash rather than <u>cards</u>.
F I <u>keep a detailed record</u> of my spending.
G I go to shops where the <u>choice is limited</u>.
H I <u>avoid</u> the shops where I am most tempted to buy things.

Speaker 1	1
Speaker 2	2
Speaker 3	3
Speaker 4	4
Speaker 5	5

Vocabulary

Phrasal verbs with *out*

1 Replace the underlined expressions with phrasal verbs with *out*. Use the correct form of the verbs.

back	run	sell	stay	take
	throw	turn	wear	

1 Plastic shopping bags can usually be re-used, so don't <u>put them in the bin</u> after one use.
2 We <u>haven't got any bread left</u> because I had lots of toast last night while you were out!
3 At first, the evening was boring but <u>it was okay in the end</u> when my uncle told some hilarious stories.
4 Henry was going to buy himself a bright orange suit but he <u>couldn't do it</u> when his friend said he looked like a tangerine.
5 Order those trainers as soon as they become available because they'll <u>all get bought</u> really quickly.
6 Mike is <u>exhausted</u> because he's been shopping all day in the city's largest mall.
7 Dilek isn't working tomorrow so she <u>isn't going to come home until</u> late tonight.
8 Now that I use my phone to pay for things, I rarely <u>get</u> money from the bank.

2 Write a word from each box in the gaps in the dialogues. There are two words you do not need.

> A: brand   catalogue   checkout
> formal   genuine   mall   trolley

> B: absurd   dreadful   furious   massive
> smart   stunning   unfashionable

1 **A:** It took me 30 minutes to get out of the supermarket because the queues for the .... were so long.
   B: That sounds (very bad) ....!
2 **A:** What I like about the new shopping .... is its huge glass dome, which fills the whole space with light.
   B: I agree – it's (really beautiful) ....
3 **A:** I never buy that .... of toothpaste because it's so expensive.
   B: Yes, I think it's (really silly) .... that it costs so much.
4 **A:** Look at the sunglasses on this website. Do you think they're .... or fake?
   B: Fake – they're too cheap and that style is really (not up to date) .... now.
5 **A:** Have you looked through this .... that came through the post? It's got some cool sweatshirts in it.
   B: Let's see … But they're (very big) ....! I prefer something tighter fitting.
6 **A:** I'm not wearing a jacket and tie because they'd be too .... for a picnic in the park.
   B: But we're going to the theatre afterwards – you need to look (well-dressed) .... for that.

Grammar

Wish and if only

 a b

1 ⊙ Some of these sentences written by exam candidates contain mistakes. Correct any mistakes.

1 I wish Grandma could to stay with us for a few more days.
2 Elaine wishes she saw the dress before her friend.
3 If only my mother could have picked me up from school when it was raining.
4 The shop had loads of great things in it, and I wish I would have been able to buy some of them.
5 When vintage clothing from an online store didn't arrive after ten days, I wished that I never ordered it.
6 My brother wishes I would let him come shopping with me, but that's not going to happen!
7 My friends and I wish the shops stayed open longer.
8 If only Matthew could win the cycling race last Saturday – it was such a close thing.
9 I wish everyone is going to wear bright, cheerful crazy clothes all the time.
10 At the weekend, I'm going away and I wish I can fit all my things in a small bag to take on the bus.

2 Complete these sentences with appropriate endings using the correct form of the verb given.

1 My flat is really tiny. I wish it .... (be)
2 I love the food they sell in that shop, but I can't afford it. If only it .... (cost)
3 My flatmate plays dreadful music really loudly all the time. I wish she .... (play)
4 My favourite brother lives too far away to visit very often. If only he .... (live)
5 I backed out of the long-distance swim because of a lack of training. I wish I .... (do)
6 My friend was looking at her phone all the time when we met up. I wish she .... (spend)
7 The band only performed new songs, which weren't as good as their big hits. If only they .... (sing)
8 The restaurant we went to last night only had a very limited choice of dishes. I wish there .... (have)

Causative *have* and *get*

3 ⊙ Some of these sentences written by exam candidates contain mistakes with causative *have* or *get*. Correct any mistakes.

1 It was September when I last have my beard cut by a barber.
2 Charlie had to get fixed his laptop last week.
3 I would love to have my paintings exhibited in a gallery.
4 I'm going to make a check to my car at a garage before the long drive.
5 I'm afraid Bradley isn't in at the moment – he's having a tooth extracted at the dentist!
6 At the festival, be careful to have not your tent stolen.
7 I always get my essays checked by a friend before I submit them.
8 I went to the beauty salon to have my nails done.
9 At the entrance to the hotel, everyone must be checked their bags.
10 Before the operation, I took my temperature by the nurse.

4 Put the words in the correct order to form questions. Then give full answers.

1 you / ears / your / have / pierced / had / ?

....

....

2 bright pink / had / you / painted / have / your kitchen / ?

....

....

3 last / did / checked / you / have / your passport / when / ?

....

....

4 have / you / do / how / your blood pressure / taken / often / ?

....

....

5 get / where / you / printed / do / your photos / ?

....

....

6 have / would / designed / to / a house / you / especially for you / like / ?

....

....

7 a contract / ever / had / you / a lawyer / checked / by / have / ?

....

....

8 by / have / this exercise / you / marked / anyone / will / ?

....

....

Reading and Use of English

Part 4

1 Read the exam task instructions and the example. Why are all the following answers wrong for the example?

1 I wish I had seen that special offer!

2 If only I saw that special offer!

3 If only I had bought something in that special offer!

4 If only you had mentioned that special offer!

2 Now do the exam task.

Need help? Go to Quick steps page 83 in the Student's Book

For questions **1–6**, complete the second sentence so that it has a similar meaning to the first sentence, using the word given. **Do not change the word given.** You must use between **two** and **five** words, including the word given. Here is an example (**0**).

Example:

0 It's a shame I didn't see that special offer!

ONLY

If ....ONLY I HAD SEEN....... that special offer!

1 I'm planning to come home before 10 o'clock this evening.

OUT

I don't plan to .... than 10 o'clock this evening.

2 These peaches are delicious – what a pity I didn't buy more of them!

WISH

I .... more of these peaches – they're delicious!

3 The film star's personal chefs cook his dinner every night.

HAS

The film star .... his personal chefs every night.

4 Unfortunately, there weren't any tickets left for the play when we tried to book seats.

ALREADY

Unfortunately, the tickets for the play .... out when we tried to book seats.

5 This printer was a bargain – it cost 40% less than usual.

OFF

This printer was a bargain because it .... its usual price.

6 Yesterday, a child's football broke the window of the bakery shop.

GOT

Yesterday, the bakery shop window .... a child's football.

Writing

1 Look at the exam task and complete the following statements.

1 You must write a minimum of .... words.
2 You are given .... points that you have to include, plus at least .... point that you have thought of yourself.
3 You must give .... for your opinions.

2 Do you think the essay statement is correct?

✅ Exam task

In your English class you have been talking about the advantages and disadvantages of buying things second-hand. Now, your English teacher has asked you to write an essay.

Write an essay using all the notes and give reasons for your point of view.

> *Buying things second-hand is better than buying new things. Do you agree?*
>
> **Notes**
> Write about:
> 1 how buying things second-hand can help the environment
> 2 things you can't buy second-hand
> 3 your own idea

Write your **essay** in **140–190** words in an appropriate style.

3 Read the model essay and answer these questions.

1 Find and number the following:
   a Point 1 from the notes
   b Point 2 from the notes
   c The writer's own idea
   d A summary of the writer's opinion on this topic
   e An idea that introduces the topic

2 Find one phrasal verb with *out* in the essay.

3 Replace the words in bold with the following extreme adjectives:

   absurd   massive   severe

4 Explain why the writer did not include contracted forms in the essay.

There is nothing new about buying things second-hand. However, whereas previously it was done by some people out of necessity, as a means of saving money, nowadays people who can afford to buy brand new things also choose the second-hand option instead.

The main reason for this is a growing awareness of the **great** harm we are doing to the environment through both the manufacturing of new things, and through the **large** amount of waste created by throwing things out after a few uses. By choosing second-hand over new, we help reduce these problems.

There are other advantages too, such as raising money for good causes when we buy second-hand from charity shops. We are also more likely to find items that are unique if we do not just purchase the latest products in normal stores, like everyone else does.

Of course, it would be **silly** to suggest we could make all our purchases second-hand. Pens, paper, soap and other toiletries must be bought new, for example. However, if we want to reduce the environmental impact of our shopping habits, buying second-hand where possible is a great place to start.

4 Plan and write your essay. Follow the instructions in the exam task.

Need help? Go to Quick steps page 84 and the Writing bank page 118 in the Student's Book

Exam information

Part/Timing	Content	Exam focus
Reading and Use of English 1 hour 15 minutes	**Part 1** A modified cloze text containing eight gaps and followed by eight multiple-choice items. **Part 2** A modified open cloze text containing eight gaps. **Part 3** A text containing eight gaps. Each gap corresponds to a word. The stems of the missing words are given beside the text and must be changed to form the missing word. **Part 4** Six separate questions, each with a lead-in sentence and a gapped second sentence to be completed in two to five words, one of which is given as a 'key word'. **Part 5** A text followed by six multiple-choice questions. **Part 6** A text from which six sentences have been removed and placed in a jumbled order after the text. A seventh sentence, which does not need to be used, is also included. **Part 7** A text, or several short texts, preceded by ten multiple-matching questions.	Candidates are expected to demonstrate the ability to apply their knowledge of the language system by completing the first four tasks; candidates are also expected to show understanding of specific information, text organisation features, tone, and text structure.
Writing 1 hour 20 minutes	**Part 1** One compulsory essay question presented through a rubric and short notes. **Part 2** Candidates choose one task from a choice of three task types. The tasks are situationally based and presented through a rubric and possibly a short input text. The task types are: • an essay • an article • a letter or email • a review • a report	Candidates are expected to be able to write using different degrees of formality and different functions: advising, comparing, describing, explaining, expressing opinions, justifying, persuading, recommending and suggesting.
Listening Approximately 40 minutes	**Part 1** A series of eight short unrelated extracts from monologues or exchanges between interacting speakers. There is one three-option multiple-choice question per extract. **Part 2** A short talk or lecture on a topic, with a sentence-completion task which has ten items. **Part 3** Five short related monologues, with five multiple-matching questions. **Part 4** An interview or conversation, with seven multiple-choice questions.	Candidates are expected to be able to show understanding of attitude, detail, function, genre, gist, main idea, opinion, place, purpose, situation, specific information, relationship, topic, agreement, etc.
Speaking 14 minutes	**Part 1** A conversation between the examiner (the 'interlocutor') and each candidate (spoken questions). **Part 2** An individual 'long turn' for each candidate, with a brief response from the second candidate (visual and written stimuli, with spoken instructions). **Part 3** A discussion question with five written prompts. **Part 4** A discussion on topics related to Part 3 (spoken questions).	Candidates are expected to be able to respond to questions and to interact in conversational English.

Answer key

UNIT 1 LIVING DAY TO DAY

Reading and Use of English

Part 7

1

1 4

2 life as a foreign student

3 A, B, C, D

2 Exam task

1 C **2** A **3** C **4** B **5** D **6** A **7** D **8** A **9** B **10** C

Grammar

1

1 Petra belongs

2 when you leave

3 *correct*

4 they sit

5 When you visit

6 The horses need

7 it is becoming

8 *correct*

2

1 end

2 's/is staying

3 don't/do not shout

4 'm/am taking

5 owns

6 'm/am trying

Listening

Part 1

1

1 seven

2 male and female

3 talking in a restaurant, chatting about the weekend, leaving a phone message, talking in a shopping centre

4 **1** plans **2** feel **3** reason **4** place

2 Exam task

1 A **2** B **3** C **4** B

Reading and Use of English

1

1 worried

2 stressed

3 attractive

4 terrified

5 unacceptable

6 surprising

7 crowded

8 enjoyable

9 disorganised

10 impressive

Part 3

2

1 an adjective

2 how people feel about something

3 a suffix

4 a spelling change: the *e* is removed before adding -*ing*

3 Exam task

1 globally

2 friendships

3 worrying

4 confidence

5 belief

6 Researchers

7 involved

8 varied

Writing

Part 2 informal email

1

1 It's to you, written by Sam, an English-speaking friend.

2 a friend who is different from you

3 She's, mate, –, she's, loads, etc., !, who's, they're, Look forward to hearing from you soon.

2

1 **1** interesting **2** known **3** unusual **4** concerned **5** takes **6** writes **7** getting

2 He has a friend called Juan who is different. Juan lives in a different country, and is more serious and passionate. Juan takes part in demonstrations, but Francisco is more focused on his studies. Francisco likes to do fun things when he is not studying.

3 Hi, Thanks, awesome, it's who's, there's, who's name's, I've, kids, He's, I'm, Juan's, guy, He's, he's, He's, he's, cool, I'm, uni, I'm, don't, stuff

UNIT 2 DIFFERING TASTES

Listening

Part 2

1

1 **1** a radio presenter, a biography of a chef

2 a 4, 7 **b** 3, 2, 9 **c** 5, 10 **d** 6 **e** 1, 8

2 Exam task

1 inspiring

2 university

3 boat

4 waiter

5 sweets

6 11/eleven weeks

7 investor

8 passion (for food)

9 hotel

10 novel

Grammar

1

1 were chatting
2 asked
3 used to look/would look/looked
4 had already started
5 didn't use
6 was washing
7 contained
8 had worked/had been working
9 had gone

2

1 was having
2 had taken
3 used to be
4 did all this start
5 were trying
6 would photograph
7 produced
8 had been selling
9 were taken
10 was

Reading and Use of English

Part 2

1

1 past tenses: past simple, past continuous, present perfect, past perfect, past continuous
2 a superlative adjective: 3
a relative pronoun: 2
two past tense forms: 4, 6, 7 and 8

2 Exam task

1 as
2 which/that
3 most
4 had
5 order
6 been
7 was
8 did

Vocabulary

1 shape
2 heart
3 fed
4 alone
5 propose
6 attracted
7 ease
8 nerves
9 side
10 touch
11 company
12 sight

Writing

Part 2 article

1

1 an article for a magazine
2 what you were celebrating, what happened at the meal

2

1 B
2 his/her grandfather's seventieth birthday
3 A restaurant meal was arranged without his knowledge, the family arrived before him, he got a surprise

3

1 For this reason
2 In the meantime
3 Before long
4 The moment
5 Once
6 Although

UNIT 3 CHANGING PLACES

Listening

Part 3

1

1 group guided cycle trips
2 3/three

2

read all the options

3 Exam task

1 H   2 D   3 A   4 F   5 C

Grammar

1

1 can't have
2 don't have to
3 should have
4 could
5 shouldn't have
6 need to
7 might have

2

1 doesn't have to/doesn't need to
2 needn't look/don't need to look
3 may/might/could
4 had to
5 could have played/might have played/may have played
6 doesn't have to/doesn't need to/needn't
7 should have written/ought to have written
8 shouldn't have/didn't need to/needn't have

Vocabulary

1

1 response to
2 in need of
3 obsessed with
4 nothing to do with
5 conscious of
6 capable of
7 with regard to
8 familiar with

2

Across: 1 community **3** volunteer **5** collaboration **7** sustainable
Down: 2 maintenance **4** initiative **6** renovated **8** adamant

Reading and Use of English

Part 1

1

1 T   2 F   3 F

2

4, 5

3 Exam task

1 D   2 B   3 A   4 B   5 C   6 B   7 B   8 A

Writing

Part 1 essay

1

1 *Should schools take their students away on trips?*
2 *yours*

2

1 They're too informal. Possible replacements: *It is, such things, really helpful.*
2 Firstly, and most importantly, Secondly, Finally, In summary.
3 *what students could learn:* second paragraph
the cost: first paragraph
your own idea: third paragraph

UNIT 4 GETTING CREATIVE

Reading and Use of English

Part 6

1

defines/describes what a scenic painter is

2 Exam task

1 E   2 F   3 B   4 A   5 G   6 C

Grammar

1 I have already bought
2 dislike sleeping
3 enough time to eat
4 have just moved
5 finished reading
6 still haven't met or haven't yet met
7 too far for us to go
8 regrets giving
9 miss being able
10 for a few years

Reading and Use of English

Part 4

1

1 five
2 affirmative sentence becomes negative: was too late → wasn't early enough

2 Exam task

1 've/have been married | for
2 hasn't/has not performed live | since
3 went on | running until
4 doesn't/does not mind | driving
5 are | too complicated
6 attempted to | to write

Listening

Part 4

1

1 F – two people
2 F – Toby's talking about his job
3 F – three answer options
4 T – see Q1
5 F – see Q3
6 T – see Q3 & 4

2 Exam task

1 C   2 C   3 A   4 C   5 C   6 A   7 A

Vocabulary

1 g   **2** a   **3** i   **4** k   **5** c   **6** j   **7** f   **8** b   **9** e   **10** l   **11** d   **12** h

Writing

Part 2 review

1

1 a place to see art
2 on an art website
3 description, what you think of it, whether you recommend it

2

a 2   **b** 1   **c** 4   **d** 3

3

nice – wonderful/fascinating/beautiful
nice – wonderful/fascinating
small – tiny
big – huge
difficult – steep
good – suitable
nice – wonderful/fascinating/beautiful

UNIT 5 MAKING YOUR WAY

Reading and Use of English

Part 7

2

1 T
2 F – it's about the past – why they chose to become doctors
3 F – you may find several
4 F – they are in random order

4 Exam task

1 B **2** D **3** A **4** C **5** A **6** D **7** C **8** D **9** A **10** B

Grammar

1 homework
2 help
3 *correct*
4 knowledge
5 *correct*
6 advice
7 rubbish
8 leisure
9 earnings
10 *correct*

Reading and Use of English

Part 3

1

1 work
2 a specific career change

2

1 a countable noun
2 plural

3

many, have

4 Exam task

1 reality
2 terrifying
3 unexpectedly
4 employment
5 impressive
6 vacancy
7 encouragement
8 trainee

Listening

Part 2

1

1 bike courier
2 a word or short phrase

2 Exam task

1 freedom
2 radio
3 (bike) lock
4 cousin
5 post room/postroom/post-room
6 empty
7 pay
8 9/nine
9 confidence
10 personal trainer

Writing

Part 2 formal letter of application

1

1 photographer's assistant, summer only
2 The couples are from around the world.
3 when you will be able to start work, how well you can speak English and any other languages, why you are interested in doing this job
4 It will be more formal.

2

1 25 **2** 6–10 **3** 3 **4** 10–12 **5** 21–24 **6** 16–20 **7** 2

3

Rob – Mr Kelly; want – would like; reckon – believe; tons of – many; etc, – and so on; I'll – I will; OK – very happy; Best wishes – Yours sincerely

4

advertisement, assistant, professional, intermediate, elementary

UNIT 6 SETTING THE PACE

Listening

Part 1

1

1 They're all different speakers.
2 She's giving advice.
3 She has backache.
4 It focuses on how he's feeling.
5 It focuses on gist.
6 It has only four questions – the exam has eight.

2 Exam task

1 C 2 B 3 C 4 B

Grammar

1

1 which we used to live in/where we used to live
2 , who won a gold medal four years ago, OR who (no commas)
3 the table which
4 documentaries, which
5 *correct*
6 know whose phone

7 *correct*

8 *correct*

9 Ricardo, who

10 the town where my mum

2

1 where

2 who I've known since I was very young, has just won

3 which/that – *could leave out*

4 who/that

5 handball, which he learnt to play at school, in the local league

6 whose

Vocabulary

1

1	dressing up	**4**	tidy up
2	staying up	**5**	used up
3	heal up	**6**	speed up

2

Across		Down	
1	prescription	**2**	recovery
5	mental	**3**	care
7	therapeutic	**4**	temperature
9	infection	**6**	stitches
10	heal	**8**	cure

Word from the shaded boxes: treat

Reading and Use of English

1	most	**5**	to
2	which	**6**	no
3	addition	**7**	What
4	of	**8**	as/like

Writing

Part 2 letter

1

1 an English-speaking friend

2 three

3 it's for a friend, it starts with Hi, it uses contractions

4 140–190

2

1 2

2 3

3 He thanks Toni for the letter and comments on what Toni is doing.

4 Hey, Hello, Dear, Love from, Best wishes

3

so (that), in order/so as

Reading and Use of English

Part 6

1

1 bamboo   **2** one

2 Exam task

1 F   **2** C   **3** B   **4** A   **5** D   **6** G

Vocabulary

2 e   **3** i   **4** a   **5** h   **6** k   **7** d   **8** b   **9** l   **10** f   **11** c   **12** j

Listening

Part 3

1

1 advice about having a more sustainable approach to clothing

2 three

3 read all the options carefully

2 Exam task

1 G   **2** A   **3** H   **4** B   **5** C

Grammar

1 if he had some qualifications

2 *correct*

3 If Diana hadn't given me a lift

4 she wouldn't have bought

5 *correct*

6 *correct*

7 she wouldn't be unemployed now

8 *correct*

9 if it hadn't run off the road just in time

10 *correct*

Reading and Use of English

Part 4

1

1 the word given

2 the meaning of the sentences

3 no – minimum of two

2

because of the meaning of the first sentence and the grammar of the second – *hadn't rained*

3 Exam task

1 wouldn't/would not | have been able

2 are | in favour of

3 is | in progress

4 even though | scientists have

5 if you have | a great

6 are used | more

Writing

Part 1 essay

1

1 140

2 The harm plastic waste does to the environment.

3 students' own answers

4 yes

2

1 While

2 However

3 Because

4 Consequently

UNIT 8 MOVING AHEAD

Reading and Use of English

Part 5

1

1 the internet causing damage to memory

2 (varying answers) A scientist will probably support the idea that the internet might be harmful.

2 Exam task

1 D **2** C **3** A **4** D **5** D **6** B

Grammar

1

1 the United States

2 have a swim

3 *correct*

4 is a very nice person

5 save energy

6 *correct*

7 protect the environment

8 I am a student

9 on the civilisation

10 Like all inventions

2

1 The photos were taken by a professional photographer.

2 The students should be asked whether they want a new hall.

3 Have your speakers been fixed yet?

4 Most music used to be recorded onto tape.

5 Pollution levels are thought to be falling.

6 The terms of the agreement have not yet been agreed by both sides.

7 The new president is expected to be Sarah James./Sarah James is expected to be the new president.

8 The new theatre will be constructed by a local company.

9 It is not known whether the new drug will cure the disease.

10 The thieves are thought to have escaped on a moped.

Reading and Use of English

Part 1

1

B

2

an opinion-based text

3 Exam task

1 B **2** B **3** A **4** C **5** D **6** C **7** A **8** B

Listening

Part 2

1

Virtual reality is when a computer produces images and sounds that make you think an imagined situation is real. It can be used for gaming, sports training, designing, education, etc.

2

a woman called Marta, a technology museum

3

1 something that a building could look like

2 a year

3 a time period

4 an activity

5 a noun (phrase), an aspect of future life

6 something she could do to help other people

7 a noun (phrase), something people have

8 people

9 something that has arms

10 a person

4 Exam task

1 mobile/cell phone

2 2017

3 a/1/one month

4 shopping

5 space travel

6 rescue

7 diseases

8 world leaders

9 robot

10 prince

Writing

1

1 for an English-language magazine called *Click!*

2 It will be published in the mazagine.

3 about something that you don't use technology for

2

1 **1** Because **2** though **3** Consequently **4** since

2 newspapers are supplied for customers

3 (varying answers) I have no problem with technology, I'm not so keen on using technology for, while I'm sipping my cappuccino, So I definitely won't be changing this habit any time soon!

UNIT 9 BREAKING NEWS

Reading and Use of English

Part 4

1 warned us (that) hiking was / warned us about hiking being
2 if I knew
3 must be researched
4 be possible to stream
5 making (the) arrangements for
6 refused to tell

Vocabulary

1

Across	Down
2 variety	1 least
5 arrangements	3 freezer
7 preferences	4 introduction
8 identities	6 appearance
9 contribution	
10 coincidence	

2

1 abilities	6 depth(s)
2 proof	7 admiration
3 death	8 amusement
4 reviews	9 intention/intent
5 length	10 reduction

Reading and Use of English

Part 3

1

1 gap 4
2 suffix: 1, 2, 3, 4, 8; prefix: 6; changes within the given word: 5, 7

2 Exam task

1 majority	5 content
2 connection(s)	6 dislike
3 commitment	7 response
4 relationships	8 involvement

Listening

Part 4

1

1 a journalist called Dr Khalid Ali, talking about the use of AI in journalism
2 artificial intelligence

2

underline:

1 why, appear
2 say, using AI to collect data
3 thinks, identify fake news
4 says, monitor comments, lead to
5 think, key advantage, graphics, AI
6 thinks, chat media
7 say, future, journalists

3 Exam task

1 C   2 B   3 B   4 A   5 C   6 A   7 A

Grammar

1 she would look
2 whether she had
3 insisted on paying
4 she had bought
5 I would get
6 threatened to expose
7 what had happened, had broken
8 us to go
9 had won
10 me not to turn on my phone

Writing

Part 2 report

1

1 a famous journalist
2 give a talk
3 what information you would like her to give in her talk, how long the talk should be, what follow-up activities students could do in class afterwards
4 140
5 formal

2

1 The aim
2 It would be interesting
3 It would be sensible
4 After the talk
5 Alternatively
6 To sum up

UNIT 10 SHOPPING AROUND

Listening

Part 3

1

how they've reduced what they buy

Possible answers:

A put off/wait
B not spend/keep
C driving me/making me
D donate/give to charity
E bank/credit/debit cards
F write down everything
G not a large range
H keep away from/don't go to

3 Exam task

1 H **2** C **3** A **4** B **5** F

Vocabulary

1

1 throw them out
2 have run out of bread
3 it turned out okay
4 backed out
5 sell out
6 worn out
7 will/is going to stay out
8 take out

2

1 checkout, dreadful
2 mall, stunning
3 brand, absurd
4 genuine, unfashionable
5 catalogue, massive
6 formal, smart

Grammar

1

1 could stay
2 she had seen
3 *correct*
4 I could have bought/had been able to buy
5 that I had never
6 *correct*
7 *correct*
8 could have won/had won
9 everyone wore bright
10 I could fit

2

Possible answers:

1 wasn't (so small)/were bigger
2 cost less/didn't cost so much
3 'd/would play better music/didn't play it
4 lived nearer
5 'd/had done more training
6 'd/had spent less time looking at it
7 'd/had sung more of their hits
8 had been more choice

3

1 I last had my beard
2 get his laptop fixed
3 *correct*
4 get/have my car checked
5 *correct*
6 not to have your tent stolen
7 *correct*
8 *correct*
9 must have/get their bags checked
10 I had my temperature taken

4

1 Have you had your ears pierced?
2 Have you had your kitchen painted bright pink?
3 When did you last have your passport checked?
4 How often do you have your blood pressure taken?
5 Where do you get your photos printed?
6 Would you like to have a house designed especially for you?
7 Have you ever had a contract checked by a lawyer?
8 Will you have this exercise marked by anyone?

Reading and Use of English

Part 4

1

1 doesn't use 'only,' the given word
2 grammatically incorrect
3 answer too long, and says more than the first sentence
4 meaning of answer is different to first sentence

2 Exam task

1 stay/be out later
2 wish I'd/had bought/got
3 has (his) dinner cooked/made/prepared by
4 had/were already sold
5 had 40% off
6 got broken by

Part 1 essay

1 140   **2** two, one   **3** reasons

1–3   see model essay below
4   The writer is using a formal style.

Model essay

e   There is nothing new about buying things second-hand. However, whereas previously it was done by some people out of necessity, as a means of saving money, now people who could afford to buy brand new things also choose the second-hand option instead.

a   The main reason for this is a growing awareness of the **severe** harm we are doing to the environment through both the manufacturing of new things, and through the **massive** amount of waste created by <u>throwing things out</u> after a few uses. By choosing second-hand over new, we help reduce these problems.

c   There are other advantages too, such as raising money for good causes when we buy second-hand from charity shops. We are also more likely to find items that are unique if we do not just purchase the latest products in normal stores, like everyone else does.

b   Of course, it would be **absurd** to suggest we could make all our purchases second-hand. Pens, paper, soap and other toiletries must be bought new, for example. However, if we want to
d   reduce the environmental impact of our shopping habits, buying second-hand where possible is a great place to start.

Audio scripts

🔊 01 **Unit 1, Listening Part 1**

You will hear people talking in four different situations. For questions 1–4, choose the best answer A, B or C.

1 *You hear a woman talking to a friend in a restaurant.*

Man: Ah, there you are!

Woman: Hi – I'm so sorry I'm late for the meal.

Man: That's OK – what happened?

Woman: It's taken me ages to get here – it would've been quicker to walk to be honest! I think there must've been an accident on the main roundabout, as everyone coming into town is having to go down George Street – even the buses and taxis – so you can imagine the effect that's having across town – nothing's moving! I think I'd better leave my car here at the restaurant and get the train home if there's still a problem when we've finished dinner. I've never seen it so bad!

2 *You hear a father and his daughter chatting about this weekend.*

Man: It's Friday at last! Don't you just love weekends?

Woman: They're great unless I've got lots of college work to do – which I haven't at the moment. Did I tell you I'd promised to go and help grandma in her garden on Sunday?

Man: No, you didn't. That's nice of you. She'll certainly keep you busy!

Woman: I know! But I've been worried about not seeing her – it's ages since I've visited, and I've missed hearing all her news. I hope she'll have baked one of her amazing cherry pies for me!

Man: Yeah, you'll need it after doing all that gardening with her!

3 *You hear a man leaving a phone message for his sister.*

Man: Hi, Louisa. Sorry I've missed you. I'm going out for the rest of the evening, so I'll leave you this message and we can chat another time. Thanks for emailing me the details of the apartment we're going to share on our city break – we really appreciate you sorting it all out. Julia and I are really looking forward to seeing you there. We'll be driving down on Wednesday afternoon, and arriving at the apartment that evening – quite early so we should be able to have dinner together. Speak soon, bye.

4 *You overhear a man and a woman talking in a shopping centre.*

Woman: Look at those running shoes in the department store window. They're in the sale – what a bargain! Let's go in and see if they've got my size.

Man: Right, but how about doing that after a coffee in their café? I could do with a rest.

Woman: Already? It's not far off lunchtime. If we wait a bit longer, we could look for somewhere to stop for a proper meal.

Man: You're obviously forgetting what great cakes they do.

Woman: I thought you just wanted a coffee! Come on, then. Let's see what they've got today. It'll be nice to sit down for a while, anyway.

🔊 02 **Unit 2, Listening Part 2**

You will hear a radio presenter reviewing a biography of a chef. For questions 1–10, complete the sentences with a word or short phrase.

My book review for the Cooking Programme this week is a biography. It's Kwame Onwuachi's *Notes from a Young Black Chef: A Memoir*. I find that many chef's biographies tend to be rather similar to each other, and sometimes not terribly interesting. But this one's different – without a doubt, it won't just be chefs who find it a really inspiring read. I'm sure anyone that picks it up will do.

Kwame Onwuachi grew up in the Bronx, New York, in a family struggling to pay the bills. Kwame didn't think much of school, and was always getting into trouble. At the age of 10, his mother sent him to live with his grandmother in Nigeria – in an attempt to change his ways. But, when he came back to New York, he got into even worse trouble during his high school years. He started a course at university, but got thrown out for behaviour that they couldn't tolerate.

After that, he left New York to go and live with his mother in Louisiana. There, he got his first job connected to cookery. Rather than taking the usual route of starting off in a restaurant kitchen, he got work cooking for the crew on a boat that was cleaning up the ocean after a huge oil spill. From then on, his life began to be transformed by the world of food. On returning to New York in 2010, he got work in a top restaurant as a waiter, working with some of the city's best chefs, and dreaming of what his future could be.

Things continued to improve for him, and he started his own catering business. To fund this, he saved money from working in a kiosk in New York's subway, where he sold sweets. He then completed a course at the Culinary Institute of America, following which he trained as a chef in some of the city's best restaurants, and competed in the TV cooking show, Top Chef.

Kwame's life did not always go smoothly, however. His book tells the story of the restaurant he opened in 2016 in Washington called Shaw Bijou, which was a complete failure. In fact, it shut after being in business a mere 11 weeks. He'd begun by serving extravagant, 13-course tasting menus, but food critics had not been convinced that it was worth the high prices he was charging. After two months, he'd reduced the prices and had been forced to change the menu, but it had been too late. The investor who'd put in most of the start-up money decided Kwame's restaurant had to be closed.

What is clear throughout this story is that there is one thing that drove Kwame, and it wasn't a desire to get away from his roots. It was a passion for food – it never left him, regardless of the ups and downs in his life, and the need to make money never became more important than that for Kwame. Now he's bounced back, and has returned to a type of home cooking, which could loosely be described as American Afro-Caribbean, influenced by his family connections to Louisiana, Jamaica, Trinidad, and Nigeria. He's still in Washington, running a hotel restaurant called Kith and Kin. And he's finally getting the praise from critics that he was so desperate for when he started out.

Next week, our book review on the Cooking Programme will be of the latest publication by leading chef of the 1990s, Mario Bonetti. You might expect a recipe book from this master of Mediterranean fine dining, but in fact it's a novel he's written, set in a restaurant in the Italian Alps. So why not read it and see if you agree with our review?

Thank you for listening. Goodbye until next week.

🔊 03 **Unit 3, Listening Part 3**

You will hear five short extracts in which people are talking about a group cycle trip they went on. For questions 1–5, choose from the list (A–H) what each speaker said about the trip they went on. Use the letters only once. There are three extra letters which you do not need to use.

Speaker 1

I've just completed a fantastic guided group bike ride in Columbia. I can't say it was easy, but that's why I went – for the challenge. Some mountain climbs were particularly hard, but when I got tired, I'd think, 'It's OK, one more kilometre then I'll stop with the guide.' A chat with her would give me a boost, then I'd feel ready to get back on the road. At other tough bits, someone from our group would pass and say something funny to cheer me up, or a truck would pass me and give me a friendly honk on the horn. Those are the things that got me through.

Speaker 2

The cycle tour I booked in Argentina was the trip of a lifetime for me. I'd wanted to go there for years, and it didn't disappoint. The success of a group trip like this depends very much on who's travelling with you, and on the bike tour I was lucky enough to join a large family of Canadians who I connected with straight away. The only other person with us was our guide, Silvio, who also became a good friend. Over dinner, we'd reflect on the day, saying that it had been the best of the trip so far. Then the next day would somehow manage to be even better!

Speaker 3

The ride I went on in China with nine other cyclists was one of the most inspiring trips ever. We rode along the Li River through a landscape that looked just like a Chinese painting. I was part of a group that included all generations, and perhaps because of this, no one felt the need to race to finish the day's route first. Most of us were happy to take our time, but it never felt too slow. If anyone got left behind, our local guide made sure we all got back together at regular stops along the way. It was demanding at times, but suitable for any experienced cyclist.

Speaker 4

Our group cycle tour was along the River Danube, which is one of the most popular routes offered by the tour company. That's because most of it's quite flat and the towns cycled through on the route are exceptionally beautiful. Plus of course, the riverside scenery is stunning, especially when the fields are full of sunflowers, as they were when I did the trip. As a consequence of all this, I'd been a bit concerned about it being very crowded. Happily it wasn't, and the fact that plenty of people use it means there are plenty of opportunities to stop and get refreshments.

Speaker 5

Last year, I went cycling in Slovenia. I joined the tour group in the capital, then we followed tracks and country lanes to the mountains. As we got higher, passing through villages and remote farms, often being greeted by the farmers with a shout or a wave, the cycling got tougher. At some points, it became so steep I had to get off and walk. But reaching the top to admire the incredible scenery below and all around us, was a reward that made us forget what had led up to it. Travelling by bike truly is a great way to explore a country.

🔊 04 **Unit 4, Listening Part 4**

You will hear a man called Toby Jackson telling a friend about his job as an animator, someone who creates pictures and makes them into cartoons or videos. For questions 1–7, choose the best answer (A, B or C).

Friend: So you're doing really well with your animations now, Toby. Tell me about your new job.

Toby: Well, as you know, after uni I did an internship, which was fantastic. The company I did that with mainly produced government information animations and doing those really gave me the technical tools I needed to get work at Donut Animations, where I am now. They're best known for doing educational videos, and most of their clients come to them for that kind of work, but they also do some commercial advertising jobs, sometimes.

Friend: So what is it you're working on at the moment?

Toby: Well, we're in the research phase of a new project at the moment. A client wants us to create a video story that involves some elephants, so I'm studying how they move and behave. Some colleagues find this part of the process a bit frustrating – they want to get on with putting the story together – but to me, this is what makes each project individual, and it's rewarding to be turning into a bit of an expert on what I'm researching.

Friend: Do you work in a large team?

Toby: No, it's small. And that's great for several reasons. Unlike in a large company, where you focus on one particular part of the creative process, here at Donut we all get to take part in major projects from start to finish. So that's through planning all the way to the final cut. You and the team get a real buzz from seeing characters you've created together developing over the weeks of the project.

Friend: Sounds great. Doing such a creative job must be really satisfying.

Toby: It is, though I find the creativity – making something no-one's ever made before – less satisfying than seeing the change in my work, both technically and artistically. As an animator, you're always getting better and adding new techniques to your repertoire. I have a portfolio of all my stuff, and looking back to the early days of my career, I can now be really critical!

Friend: And the job must be a lot of fun, too.

Toby: Well yes. A sense of fun's essential for a good animator. But even if you have that in spades, a client may give you a really dull topic and you'll struggle to find a way to make it amusing. Or when you're under stress, working all night to complete a comedy animation on time – the fun is harder to achieve then. You have to stop and play a silly game or something to get in the right mood.

Friend: And I guess you're always starting new projects – what's that like?

Toby: Well, it takes me a while to get into them. As soon as the company takes on our next project, the creative director, Rachel, is brilliant at coming up with all sorts of great ideas straightaway. I'm much slower, but once an idea's been suggested, I'm one of the best at building the story around it.

Friend: Right. And I guess you use new technology, don't you?

Toby: Absolutely. New software is becoming available all the time – and we have to use as much of this as possible because it makes such a difference to the finished product. Recent developments give animators incredible freedom – we've reached the point where anything that we can possibly think up, we can make into an animation. It's amazing!

Friend: Wow! I'd love to see some of your work.

🔊 **05** Unit 5, Listening Part 2

You will hear a woman called Leila Osman talking on a podcast about working as a bike courier in London. For questions 1–10, complete the sentences with a word or short phrase.

Hi, I'm Leila Osman. I'm a bike courier in London – I collect and deliver letters and parcels by bike.

Many people say they'd hate my job because of the traffic and the weather, but most of the time I love it. One reason it suits me is the cycling, a passion of mine which also helps maintain my fitness. But what I'd rank top of all the job's advantages is the freedom I have – I'm in charge of my working day, and that's priceless.

I'm self-employed, but I get as much work as I want from just one courier company. They also supply me with some of the kit I need, such as a radio. I need that so they can contact me with details of jobs. I have to provide my own bag, which I carry all the items for delivery in, and the waterproof jacket I wear is one I bought myself, too.

My bike isn't anything special but it's easy to ride. I decided against anything too pricey because of the risk of it being stolen. I work in some rough areas, so I invested in a top-of-the-range bike lock. I spent a fortune but it was worth it to get something strong but not heavy. There's little point in getting things like expensive bike lights, as they too often get taken or broken.

The other crucial thing that bike couriers have to carry around is a tyre repair kit. I'm an expert at repairing tyres nowadays, but when I started, I used to get a colleague to help me. Then I got my cousin to show me how to do it properly, and it's never been a problem since.

At the beginning of each day, I call the courier company, get instructions for the first item to pick up, and cycle to wherever it is. If it's a small building, I normally head straight in through the front door to reception. But if it's a huge, glass office block, I'll go in through the service entrance at the back, and then find the post room, where I'll pick up my package.

I then deliver the package, go and collect the next one and continue this routine until I have no packages left, and nothing to collect. Then I contact the courier company to let them know. What I actually say to them is that I'm 'empty' – then they know to send me through some more jobs. If there isn't anything to do, they'll put me on what they call 'stand by' until another job's available.

When I'm waiting for more jobs, I can do whatever I want to. Often, I meet up with another bike courier to have coffee and we chat about how awful certain aspects of the job are. The most common topic is pay – it's pretty bad in this job. Most customers are reasonable, but every courier has at least one funny story to tell about them.

Being self-employed, I can choose how many hours I put in each day. Most couriers do between seven and ten. I do nine as a rule, but I sometimes do ten, like when colleagues are off sick. A couple of years ago, I occasionally did 12 hour days – that was awful!

I feel quite comfortable in the job now. I've built up a good level of stamina, which means I can work all day, and I've still got energy to go out in the evening and see friends. I've also gained a lot of confidence in cycling in heavy traffic. That was difficult for me, as I was brought up in a quiet village.

However. It's not a job you can do forever. Most people do it as a temporary thing when they're young, and I'm no different. I've thought about starting my own delivery company – being the business owner for a change, but I think I'd prefer to be a personal trainer. That would use all the things I'm best at, I think. But I won't stop the bike courier job just yet …

🔊 **06** Unit 6, Listening Part 1

You will hear people talking in four different situations. For questions 1–4, choose the best answer A, B or C.

1 *You hear a running coach giving advice about the week before a marathon.*

There are various things that can go wrong for you in the last week before running a marathon. One is panic setting in, caused by a realisation that you haven't done enough training, and fear of injury resulting from that. Obviously, it's too late to do much about how physically prepared you are, except stay calm and tell yourself that you can still get through the race successfully. Come to terms with your actual level of fitness and what that'll allow you to achieve. Whatever you do, don't force yourself to complete a long 20-mile training run. That certainly won't help you complete the race.

2 *You hear a woman phoning her daughter about an arrangement for tonight.*

Woman: Hi Katie – would you mind if I came to dinner another night?

Daughter: Oh dear – what's up, Mum? Is it your back again?

Woman: Yes. It's not too bad but because I've been painting the sitting room today, it's feeling a bit stiff now. I just don't want to risk making it as bad as it was last year, so I think I should probably stay here and take it easy. I've taken some paracetamol, which has helped, and I'm going for a lie down. Sorry to mess up our plans.

Daughter: Sounds very sensible, Mum. We can easily do dinner tomorrow or the day after.

Woman: Great, thanks Katie.

3 *You hear a man talking about a change in his diet.*

I've completely cut out fast food, caffeine and anything highly processed or high in sugar. I know it's going to be good for me in the long run, but I'm struggling with it at the moment. Giving up sugar is much harder than I imagined it would be, and my body's still adjusting to it. I'm experiencing periods during the day when I can't be bothered to do anything, and then, I really miss that immediate boost I used to get from a chocolate bar or fizzy drink – even though it never used to last long! At least I'm sleeping better at night, though.

4 *You hear a woman giving advice to footballers about looking after their feet.*

Football can put a lot of stress on the feet, especially when you're playing on hard surfaces such as artificial turf. Your boots may also be putting added pressure on various parts of your feet, and it's not unusual for a footballer to damage the skin on his or her feet, as well as their toenails. Players have different preferences in terms of design and the material they're made from and so on, but a good quality, well-fitting pair of boots is essential. There shouldn't be any signs of strain on the foot after a game or training session.

You will hear five short extracts in which people are giving advice about taking a more sustainable approach to clothes. For questions 1–5 choose from the list (A–H) what advice each speaker gives. Use the letters only once. There are three extra letters which you do not need to use.

Speaker 1

In today's era of 'fast fashion', the availability of cheap fashionable clothes encourages people to buy whatever they take a fancy to without much thought. This is bad news for the environment, mainly because of the huge amounts of waste it creates. When you enter a shop, rather than grabbing clothes just because they're a bargain, or they're new in, you should only get what you intended to buy before going in. This requires an investment of time and thought to find out the best place to get what you want, and ensure it's somewhere that takes environmental concerns seriously.

Speaker 2

Many people's wardrobes are full of clothes that are loved but never worn, which is such a wasted resource. If you have items like these, think about why you like them – is it the colour? The fabric? The fit? And then consider why you never wear them. It will often be possible to keep the positives and do something about the negatives, like dying things a different colour, or altering the sleeves on a shirt so they're a better shape for you. You'll have new clothes without having to buy them, thereby saving yourself money at the same time as helping the environment.

Speaker 3

There's a lot of talk nowadays about what the fashion industry should be doing to clean up their act, but I'm a firm believer it's consumers like you and me that can make change happen. By choosing to buy only clothing made with little impact on the environment, we force manufacturers to alter their processes. But this means being tough when you go shopping. Refuse to be put off by sales staff who get irritated when you start asking them lots of questions, or spend ages looking at clothing labels, or checking on your phone to make sure the brand has a good reputation on environmental issues.

Speaker 4

One way of being a 'greener' consumer is to buy fewer clothes, which may mean you'll be able to afford more expensive designer brands. However, if you're willing to put in a bit of work, you can keep cheaper items in usable condition for many years, too. Small rips and holes in clothing fabric can often be sewn up and missing buttons can be sewn back on. For little expense, a shoe with a heel snapped off it can be taken to a cobbler, who will return it to you looking as good as new. In this way, you avoid creating unnecessary waste, and you might even enjoy the creativity involved!

Speaker 5

When I go clothes shopping, I have a rather unusual way of deciding whether or not I should buy something. I ask myself, 'Would my grandma buy this?' My grandma has excellent taste, and I respect her view on most things. She always says she'll only buy something new if she can see herself wearing it again and again, and possibly at some point giving it away to a charity shop selling second-hand clothing. It's a great guiding principle for clothes shopping: never buy stuff you'd throw away or that would fall apart after you'd worn it a couple of times.

You will hear a woman called Marta talking about a technology museum. For questions 1–10, complete the sentences with a word or short phrase.

I regularly go to South Korea's capital, Seoul, as a travel journalist, but yesterday was my first visit to its amazing technology museum. The Korean telecommunications company, SK Telecom, have created the museum in their headquarters building. I expected this to be hugely tall, but city laws limit building height to ensure views of the mountain peaks around Seoul aren't spoilt. It's built in the shape of a mobile phone to reflect its owner's business.

The museum originally opened in 2008 with two zones: 'Dream' and 'Play'. Being a technology museum, however, it has to be updated regularly, and it closed in 2016 for a major renovation. Visitors returned in 2017, when it re-opened with two new zones called 'Present' and 'Future', which imagines the world of 2050.

This is not the kind of museum where you just turn up and go in. Entry's free, but all visitors must book a tour in advance. You can do this as far ahead as a month before going, and their website says you can reserve a tour place as little as 30 minutes beforehand. However, I tried for three days before I could get a slot, so don't leave booking to the last minute.

My tour group was guided first to the Present Zone, where we experienced SK Telecom's current technologies. I found these fascinating – I couldn't believe all these technologies are in use now! For example, we put on a virtual reality headset and it took us shopping, which was fun – you really felt like you were there. We also had a ride in a self-driving car.

In the Future Zone, it gets even more mind-boggling! You enter a high-tech city called Highland, which is divided up into rooms that use various technologies to explore what future reality might be like. Some of the rooms show what global warming might do to our world, and others focus on global communication. The room I was most interested in focused on space travel. It really opened my eyes to what might become possible years from now.

As we went through the incredible rooms, we were put into teams and given missions to accomplish. First, we had to locate survivors of a wildfire, and organise a rescue. We were shown how to use images being taken by satellites to find the location of the fires in real time, right at that moment.

Our mission in the medical room was to get advice from a doctor. Not a human doctor, though, a computer programmed with AI – artificial intelligence. We also learnt how computer programmes will be able to tell you what diseases you're most likely to get. They'll be able to do this through an analysis of your genes.

As the tour continued, it became increasingly clear how great the future could be, and how everything and all nationalities could be linked through technology. We were shown world leaders coming together in a kind of virtual reality, a 'hologram'. This technology will make them appear to be attending in person, but they won't have to travel a single kilometre from their own offices, and can meet at very short notice if necessary.

At the end of the tour, we had a lot of fun in the 'Teleport Room'. There, we wore virtual reality devices to complete various tasks through simulated situations, like travelling to another planet. When I looked through the virtual reality device, I felt like a real astronaut, and my arms looked like they belonged to a robot – they made whatever movement I made in the virtual situation. We had buttons to press too, so it was a bit like a game.

As we left, I chatted with other visitors in my tour group. We all agreed the tour had been too short – none of us had wanted it to finish. One said the guide had told her a story about a prince who'd been to the museum. He'd been so impressed with what it showed that he wanted to find an architect who could build him a home with all the same technology in it!

I can totally understand why!

🔊 **09** **Unit 9, Listening Part 4**

You will hear a radio interview with a media expert called Dr Khalid Ali, who talks about the use of artificial intelligence in journalism. For questions 1–7, choose the best answer (A, B or C).

Interviewer: On today's media show, we welcome Professor of Media Studies, Doctor Khalid Ali. He's going to discuss journalism and AI. That's artificial intelligence: computer systems that can 'think', learn and problem-solve like humans. Welcome, Dr Ali.

Dr Ali: Thank you.

Interviewer: I know you were keen to come on the show and talk to our audience – can you tell us why?

Dr Ali: Yes – I really believe this subject is important to all of us, because journalism's vital to a proper understanding of our world. I want to make sure as many people as possible know about the latest developments. When we refer to automated journalism, people think we're talking about a science fiction world many years from now. Wrong. Artificial intelligence is being used here and now – I'm not sure people generally realise that.

Interviewer: OK, so let's start with something easy: data collection. Obviously, computers are great at collecting data.

Dr Ali: Absolutely. And AI programmes can monitor hundreds of news sources, and then collect relevant data. It then categorises and tags the data, so journalists can almost instantly find what they want from ever-expanding amounts of material. In this way, news organisations are simply doing what every other industry is doing: making their processes more efficient using AI.

Interviewer: Right. I've also read about AI being used to identify fake news.

Dr Ali: Yes, which is an excellent use of AI. Online platforms like Facebook use it to check facts really quickly, and to spot sentence patterns typical of fake news items. AI programmes are improving all the time, but are still best used for this purpose with some human input. Maybe in the future they'll be fully automated, but that's a way off yet.

Interviewer: OK. And can AI identify other negative elements, like inappropriate comments on news websites?

Dr Ali: It can. Many news organisations ask for comments after certain articles, and this encourages readers to engage with the news and journalists. However, you need a lot of time and money to fund the monitoring of such comments features in order to remove anything that's an offensive attack rather than an opinion on the article. Using AI allows the comments feature to be extended to a greater number of articles because fewer human monitors are required.

Interviewer: But what about providing content for articles? I believe AI tools can produce graphics from data, for example?

Dr Ali: Yes. Great for statistics. An AI tool could gather information about the popularity of a politician, let's say, and present it in nice, readily understood graphic form, with images and data combined. The real beauty of such a tool is that it can put together and present a much richer and better-connected display of information than you'd get in a simple table or chart. And it'd take much less time doing it than a human, of course.

Interviewer: Great. And can you tell us about chat media in journalism?

Dr Ali: So how that works is, instead of you finding a ready-made article, AI chat media tools start messaging you about what you want to know. It's in the early stages of development for news organisations but my guess is that it'll take off soon. Already, some newspapers have AI tools that chat to a limited extent. For example, they'll ask you which part of the world you're interested in.

Interviewer: Amazing! But how do journalists feel about computers doing their jobs?

Dr Ali: Let me stress that AI developments in journalism do not mean the end of human journalists. Certain tasks will be done by computers rather than humans, but I imagine the news room of the future will remain a collaboration between intelligent machines and humans. Rather than having less to do, journalists will have extra responsibilities connected to maintaining their AI tools.

Interviewer: Dr Ali, thank you very much.

🔊 **10** **Unit 10, Listening Part 3**

You will hear five short extracts in which people are talking about how they have reduced the number of things they buy. For Questions 1–5, choose from the list (A–H) how each person has reduced the number of things they buy. Use the letters only once. There are three extra letters which you do not need to use.

Speaker 1

Most of the time, I don't feel driven to buy things – I'm quite careful with my money. However, there are some places that I just cannot leave empty-handed. For example, there's a couple of boutiques in my town, both owned by a friend. As she knows me so well, she knows exactly what I like. So she gets stock in with me in mind, which makes it impossible for me to resist. The only thing I can do is limit myself to very occasional visits. Doing that has been a very effective way to reduce my shopping bills.

Speaker 2

When I decided to reduce the amount I was buying, I knew I had to stop buying things on impulse. I used to grab anything that caught my eye, especially in charity shops. So I ended up with loads of unused, unwanted stuff. I've managed to stop this behaviour in a remarkably simple way. When I feel tempted to buy something in a shop, I ask myself why. Is it just because I'm bored, or I've got some money, or I want to distract myself from a problem? Often, a chat with a friend, exercising or listening to music will be much more satisfying than making that purchase.

Speaker 3

I've recently developed an effective strategy for reducing the amount of money I spend online. I'd noticed that sometimes I wasn't actually bothered if I couldn't complete an order, like when it wouldn't accept my credit card details or the webpage froze. I'd completely forget about whatever it was I'd been attempting to buy. However, if I persevered with the order, that proved I really wanted or needed the item. So now, I choose something, bookmark it, and leave it for a few days. If I then still want to buy it, I feel confident it'll be a worthwhile purchase. I've cut my monthly spend by about fifty percent.

Speaker 4

My strategy for reducing the amount I buy involves a kind of mental control. Every few months I write down in my diary a target purchase, which will be something that I can't afford to buy immediately, but is something I really want. This might be dance lessons, or something for my flat. Then, when I'm tempted by something in a storefront window, I remind myself of what I really want to spend my money on. I've found it really works: not only do I buy a lot less, but what I do buy means more to me.

Speaker 5

I recently decided to make a determined effort to buy less. I'd built up some debt on credit cards, yet couldn't see where the money had gone. I needed to find out what was going on with my finances. So now, I make a note of every single item I buy, from a newspaper to a sofa, and its price. Doing this shows it's not OK to say to yourself, 'That's only a pound, I'll get it' – even small purchases add up. I also list things I almost buy, but manage to resist. That makes me feel I'm saving money, which gives me a bigger buzz than actually buying something.

Acknowledgements

The authors and publishers would like to thank the following contributors:
Grammar on the move: Lucy Passmore and Jishan Uddin

This coursebook is informed by the Cambridge English Corpus - a multi-billion word collection of examples of spoken and written English. We use our corpus to answer questions about English vocabulary, grammar and usage. Along with this, we collect and analyse learner writing. This allows us to clearly see how learners from around the world are similar and different in how they acquire and use language. These insights allow us to provide tailored and comprehensive support to learners at all stages of their learning journey.

The authors and publishers acknowledge the following sources of copyright material and are grateful for the permissions granted. While every effort has been made, it has not always been possible to identify the sources of all the material used, or to trace all copyright holders. If any omissions are brought to our notice, we will be happy to include the appropriate acknowledgements on reprinting and in the next update to the digital edition, as applicable.

Key: U = Unit

Photography

The following images have been sourced from Getty Images.

U1: FatCamera/E+; Cavan Images; xavierarnau/E+; Tony Anderson/DigitalVision; **U2:** The Washington Post; William Henry Fox Talbot/Hulton Archive; Alexander Spatari/Moment; LindaJarrett/500px; Stella Kalinina; **U3:** coberschneider/RooM; NickyLloyd/E+; Roberto Moiola/Sysaworld/Moment; Alistair Berg/DigitalVision; **U4:** Alistair Berg/DigitalVision; Cavan Images; **U5:** skynesher/iStock/Getty Images Plus; Neustockimages/E+; **U6:** Jupiterimages/Stockbyte; MIGUEL MEDINA/AFP; Shilpa Harolikar/Moment; **U7:** Westend61; Larina Marina/iStock/Getty Images Plus; **U8:** PeopleImages/E+; gilaxia/E+; **U9:** urbazon/E+; KTSDESIGN/SCIENCE PHOTO LIBRARY/Science Photo Library; skynesher/E+; **U10:** Betsie Van der Meer/DigitalVision; Jackyenjoyphotography/Moment; Maskot.

Front cover photography by Betsie Van Der Meer/Stone/Getty Images.

Animations

Grammar animation Video production by QBS Learnings. Voiceover by Dan Strauss.

Audio

Audio production by IH Sound LTD.

Typesetting

Typeset by Hyphen S.A.